D1380544

# Alone I Fly

# Alone I Fly

Bill Bailey

Pen & Sword
**AVIATION**

First published in
Great Britain in 2009
By Pen and Sword Aviation
An imprint of
Pen and Sword Books Ltd
47 Church Street
Barnsley
South Yorkshire
S70 2AS

ISBN 978-1-84884-165-9

A CIP record for this book is available from the British Library

Typeset in 11/14pt Palatino
by Mac Style, Beverley, E. Yorkshire

Printed and bound in Great Britain
by CPI UK

Pen and Sword Books Ltd incorporates the imprints of Pen and Sword Aviation, Pen and Sword Maritime, Pen and Sword Military, Wharncliffe Local History, Pen and Sword Select, Pen and Sword Military Classics and Leo Cooper.

For a complete list of Pen & Sword titles please contact
PEN & SWORD BOOKS LIMITED
47 Church Street, Barnsley, South Yorkshire, S70 2AS, England
E-mail: enquiries@pen-and-sword.co.uk
Website: www.pen-and-sword.co.uk

# CONTENTS

# About the Author

Bill Bailey is a retired schoolmaster and journalist. Amongst his many achievements, he has been editor of a national magazine and an Educational Correspondent for the B.B.C. Earlier publications include a children's book on meteorology entitled 'Weather for Kids', published by McDonalds, and printed in five languages, and an audio package entitled 'Science through Story'.

Since retiring, Bill has written a further two books, presently published in e-book format. The first, entitled 'Buying a Farm in Spain', is a non-fiction account about a UK police detective who sells up and moves to Spain. 'Buying a Farm in Spain' deals with all the problems & hassles the detective encounters while pursuing his dream. The second book, called 'Sex, Royalty and Family Life' is a biographical history of George III and his extended family. Both these books are available from www.lulu.com.

'Alone I Fly' is an account of Bill's early life and has been a labour of love over many years.

# Acknowledgements

I would like to thank my son-in-law Ronnie for all his technical assistance. Also my daughter Nicolette for holding my hand.

I must thank my wife Gwen for permission to record our love affair that has now gone on for over sixty-five years.

Finally, I would like to mention my old friends Pam and Harold Rowling for their supreme confidence in me.

# I Arrive in Egypt

The heat had hit me hard as I'd stepped off the plane at Heliopolis airport. The Pan-Am flight from Khartoum had been pressurised and cool and it had been nice to be a passenger for the very first time, but now as my fellow travellers hustled away I felt alone and isolated.

Nervously, I gazed around the reception area, for I couldn't believe that I could be there alone in Egypt in 1942.

Of course others saw me as Sergeant Pilot Bill Bailey, but I knew that I hadn't changed at all. I had rubbed my stripes in the dust to make myself look like an old hand but no one was fooled, for my bright new wings upon my neat and tidy blouse advertised my inexperience to all and sundry.

"You look lost, mate."

I turned with relief at the sound of a friendly voice, to see a chap in army battledress wheeling a great pile of wooden crates towards the door.

"Well, I'm not exactly lost," I replied. "Where are you bound?"

"I'm supposed to be reporting to 104 Squadron." He stopped his trolley and thought for a minute.

"I've never heard of 'em. Tell you what. You should report to the R.T.O. at Cairo railway station. He'll know what to do."

That seemed a sensible idea to me.

"Yes, I'll do that," I said. "Can you direct me?" The soldier grinned. "You'd have a hell of a walk from here. Why don't you hitch a lift with one of the army drivers outside? Nearly all of them will be going past the station."

So within an hour I found myself outside the R.T.O.'s office on platform 3. As I stood there, I wondered whether I should knock or just go in, but the plain fact was that I was scared. I was reporting for duty to my squadron for the first time. Maybe I would be "dicing with death" very soon, but at that moment I was worried about the niceties of knocking on the door, or walking in.

"You can't travel on tonight. Report tomorrow at 10:00 hours. The corporal i/c (in charge of) mail from 104 reports here every day and he'll take you off to the landing ground."

"But where shall I stay the night?"

"That's easy." A phone rang in the background.

"At the Combined Services Club. Sergeant, show this chap the way to the Club." He picked up the phone and left me to the guidance of the sergeant.

As I sat on the balcony of the club toying with my fruit salad and ice cream, two and a half piastres at the counter, I thought back to the strange circumstances that had led me there. The last time I had been in Cairo I was a deck-boy on the R.M.S. *Otranto* bound for Australia, and I remembered that even then the noise of the traffic was overwhelming; everyone seemed to delight in making so much din. The yellow-painted taxis drove past or stopped at the club and it didn't make much difference, for they all seemed to have trouble with their horns as though they were jammed on. Every driver of every car, van or lorry would engage in a heated slanging match every time the traffic stopped, and if by any chance the snarl-up was caused by a red traffic light, then they would all put their arms out of the window to bang out a tattoo against the body work, until the sheer volume of noise made the red light turn pale and then green with embarrassment.

It seemed strange that here I was, a sergeant pilot in the R.A.F., and yet without an educational qualification to my name.

I had been delighted to receive instructions to report to the Air-crew Selection Centre in Oxford; but when I arrived, to my dismay I was told the date was wrong and I was due the next week.

"But, Sergeant", I said, "It is the letter that is wrong and not me, and it's been a hell of a cross-country journey."

He looked at his notes.

"Fair enough, after all it is our mistake. Go on in and I'll move your name onto today's list."

The morning was spent in medical examinations and I was pretty sure I was O.K. on that score. After this, we were told to go away and come back in the afternoon for the educational tests. My heart sank, for what chance had I with all these undergrads? I had left a village school at 13 without any secondary education. You can imagine my delight when I returned to hear the sergeant say,

> "We are running a little late, and as you are all undergraduates from Oxford colleges we have decided that giving you educational tests is a waste of time. So, if you wait here, you will be called in one at a time for your interview."

My name beginning with "B" meant that I was one of the first to go before the Board. I was ushered in to find three high-ranking officers sitting at a long table.

"Oh, Bailey," said the President, looking up from his papers, "I see you have put down specifically as *pilot*. Why did you do that?"

Crossing my fingers behind my back I said "Because, sir, all my life I have wanted to fly."

The officer on his right picked up a black plastic model of an aircraft from the collection in front of him.

"In that case I am sure you can tell me what this is?"

Just at that moment the phone rang and I was removed from the room. Having spent all my time at sea, I had no idea what the plane was until the corporal told me it was a Sunderland. I was sure as I stood outside the door that I was going to be tripped up at the last hurdle; however, when I went back in I was told that I had been selected.

I thought of how I came to be there on that noisy evening. I was just another newly-fledged pilot, who, like many others, had flown a Wellington bomber across the centre of Africa and then up the Nile valley to avoid enemy attack. It still seemed a hell of a long way round. But my trouble was that things seemed to go wrong around me. Even at home you could bet your socks that it would be me that spilt the tea or broke the cups, for I seemed to have a strange attraction for disaster.

But was it always my fault when things went wrong? Was it my fault that I had been stuck in Khartoum with malaria while the others went on?

And yet Cairo seemed different at night, and as I looked across the veranda I realised I would willingly trade the exotic silhouette of domes and minarets, and the elegant promenade of palm trees, for the bare swollen outline of the North Downs and the winter tracery of an elm tree with its top hamper of rooks' nests.

I reported to the R.T.O. the next day as instructed, but there was no sign of any postman, and so I sat watching the never-ending stream of taxis sweeping round to deposit Air Force officers, Navy jobs heavy with gold braid, and dusty-faced pongoes, on the steps of Cairo Central railway station. As I leant against the hot sandstone pillar, I wondered idly what the honourable gent on the plinth in the centre of the square thought of all this frenetic activity. Maybe he was more worried about the pigeons than all the erratic traffic.

I looked up as a shadow blocked out the glare of the sun.

"Sgt. Bailey? R.T.O. says you're for 104 Squadron. I'm Stevens, the corporal i/c mail." He was dapperly dressed in khaki shirt and shorts, with his long socks turned over neatly. He reminded me of an old picture of Baden-Powell in one of my school books. He was much older than the normal airman, and was wearing medal ribbons that I knew were similar to those worn by my Dad on Armistice Day.

"I deliver the post. The jeep's just round the corner. Let's pile your stuff in the back and then we'll be on our way."

As good as his word, he grabbed my two kit-bags and marched across the concourse, brushing aside the native porters with their mountainous loads of suitcases. For one moment I felt panic. I must follow at all costs. Quickly I picked up my other bag and my aircrew holdall and dashed off in pursuit.

Soon we were weaving through the traffic making for the Alexandria road. As we drove along I did not realise that the corporal was eyeing me carefully as he drove. I was not aware that the corporal nursed a grudge against air-crew. Young brats, he considered, who pretended they were God's gift to civilisation, while strong reliable people with a sense of discipline and World War I experience were rotting away driving a blasted jeep.

*Still, thought the corporal, I can get my own back in a little way. All the air-crews travel to the field with me and this gives me a chance to keep them humble, to cut them down to size. I noticed the clean wings and grinned to myself as I realised another victim was at my mercy.*

*Already guessing the answer, I began my third degree.*

*"Been on ops before?"*

*"No."*

*"How come you've no crew?"*

*"I went down with malaria and they went on without me," the sprog replied, embarrassed.*

*"Flown Wimpies before?"*

*"Yes, I was captain on the trip out and before that it was O.T.U. at Harwell. About 60 hours, I should think."*

*I glanced at him with contempt. Hardly wet behind the ears. No wonder Rommel was getting all his own way.*

*"Pegasus or Merlins?"*

*"Pegasus."*

*I nodded in satisfaction. "Better, I reckon. Do you know, I've seen a Wimp return with so much bloody flak inside, it sounded like an over-heated sausage machine. Still it worked – now them Merlins, they get one bullet in the glycol tank and they've had it."*

*I glanced at him with a grin, for it was obvious that he was scared.*

*"Had many casualties recently?" he asked.*

*I decided not to answer directly; just stared ahead and concentrated on my driving. I knew what he was feeling and was enjoying my moment of power.*

*"I expect you'll be on ops right away."*

*I took my time, leisurely driving through the gears as I accelerated along the flat straight Alex road.*

*"I know for a fact," I said, "that they're three pilots short. Why, I seem to spend more time ferrying up pilots than I do collecting letters, d'you know what I mean?"*

*I'm sure he did know what I meant and I could see him searching feverishly for a way of changing the subject.*

*"What's the aerodrome like – the accommodation? Is it O.K.?"*

*"Tents".*

*"Did you say tents?"*

*"Yes, it's only desert with a few tents around." "How long have you been there?"*

*"Three weeks. Before that we were at Kabrit on the Bitter Lakes. Do you know it?"*

*He shook his head.*

*"No, of course not. You're new out here."*

*Well that was an established aerodrome. Quite nice that was. We used to have E.N.S.A. parties every week until we were chucked out by some crappy American squadron".*

*"What type of aircraft are they with 104?"*

*"Peggies mostly. They've got one or two Merlins but all the 4,000-pounders are Peggies." "What's a 4,000-pounder?"*

*"For Christ's sake don't you know?"*

*He shook his head, so I settled down to explain.*

*"104 Squadron are equipped to carry 4,000-pound bombs. They are very experimental, see, and each aircraft carries one bomb. What they've done is to rip out the bomb-beam and the bottom of the aircraft, and the bomb is winched up so that the outer case becomes the bottom of the plane. Do you understand what that means?"*

*"I've no idea."*

*"It means that if the undercart folds on you, then you have to belly-land by skidding at 90 mph on the outer case of the bomb."*

*"But that should be all right I should think, providing the bomb hadn't been fused."*

*I laughed scornfully.*

*"Don't you believe it," I said ... "Why, the case is so thin they go off even though they're not primed. One went off last week – took off – one engine failed – tried to land and ... curtains. I can show you the hole when we get there."*

*I really was enjoying this. It was my effort for the morale of the squadron, so I drove on while conversation lapsed.*

*"Is that the landing ground?"*

*"No, that's an American squadron. D'you know they travel daily to the U.K.? Bloke I knew had a '48' and went home and back in that time. Hitched a lift you see. No, our ground is about five miles further on."*

Soon it became obvious to me that we were approaching our destination. Wellington aircraft, the sun sparkling upon their plastic astrodomes, stood menacingly in circular enclosures made bomb-proof by boulder walls. Midget mechanics in white overalls swarmed all over the ugly black shapes, repairing the damage of the night before and grooming them for the work that was to follow.

Some aircraft I thought were beautiful, but Wellingtons with the black fabric stretched over the fuselage looked like black flying slugs. I was fascinated to see an object that looked like four oil drums welded end to end.

"Is that a 4,000-pound bomb?"

"Yeah, that's right. Not much like an ordinary bomb, is she?"

A few minutes later we turned off the road on to a track that bumped its way through a collection of tents; and soon I was saluting in front of my Flight Commander.

Flight-lieutenant De Courcy looked up at the spotty young airman.

"Glad to welcome you, Sergeant. You've come at a very useful time. Let me see now. How many hours have you done on Wimps?"

"About 60, sir."

"I see. Well, we've got to fix you up with a crew. It would be nice if you could fly for a while with someone with experience." He studied the blackboard behind him that was covered with chalky names and figures.

"Frenchie Stevens, that's the man. His crew are very experienced. In fact they are almost time-expired. His second pilot has just gone sick, so you would fit in there very well." He returned to the table and I saw a worried frown appear.

"There is only one snag, and that is that they are on readiness tonight. That's pretty rough on you. Have you travelled far today?"

"I spent the night in Cairo, sir."

"Oh good, then that's not too bad. How do you feel about doing an op tonight?" I could feel my hand shaking. This was it. As in a dream, I could hear myself saying that I was ready to go.

"Good man, then I'll take you to your tent. Every crew has its own tent in this God-forsaken hole." I followed him past tent after tent. They were all the same, I noticed: ex-World War I bell tents. However, I had never seen them half-buried in sand before. We went down three steps under the flap and found ourselves blinking in the gloom. In fact, after the glare of the sun, it seemed quite dark.

"Here you are, Frenchie. Your new second pilot." I shook hands with a shadowy figure.

"Welcome aboard," he said. "I'm Frenchie, the skipper of this motley crew. I'm not French but Canadian, from Toronto, but the ignorant bastards out there don't seem to know the difference. That sandy-haired job with the walrus moustache is Roy the navigator. Called that because his real name is Rogers ... And that's our wireless op, Aussie. Believe it or not, he comes from Australia, from Melbourne actually. And those two idiots over there are Nipper and Napper, our Cockney air-gunners." I was glad of the dark, for it hid my embarrassment. Why did I feel uncomfortable when introduced to strangers? I was conscious that someone was talking while I was shaking hands. A blinding light suddenly illuminated the tent as the Flight Commander left; then it was dark again, and cool like a brewer's cellar.

"You've probably had nothing to eat. Come on, sit down. You can use Chalky's irons. He's in hospital in Alex. And probably chatting up the nurses at the moment."

"Lucky devil," grunted the man called Nipper.

The food was quite good, corned-beef hash with tinned new potatoes followed by tinned apricots; and yet it had a strange gritty taste.

"It's the sand, gets everywhere. Sometimes in a storm you can have an inch of mud in your tea."

And then the conversation lapsed and I finished my meal in silence. My eyes were getting used to the gloom by now and I could begin to take stock of the other members of the crew.

I was impressed with Roy and felt happy and confident in his presence. He was older than the others and seemed to say, "Calm down, we can sort this out, you'll see".

The others were wrapped up in their own affairs, writing, sorting over letters. There was a tension about the tent that I was beginning to sense. I turned to the navigator.

"What do I do with the tins?"

Leave them. Its Aussie's turn and he never starts until we clobber him."

I felt in my pocket for my cigarettes. "Anyone like a fag?"

"Not Victory V's, I hope!"

"No, Player's."

"Good, then we'll all have one."

Feeling a little easier, I turned to one of the gunners.

"What does it mean to be 'time-expired'?"

"Smashin'," he said, "it's absolutely 'bang on' ."

"What does it mean?"

"It means, mate, that you've made it."

"I'll tell you," interrupted the navigator. "You see, we all have to do 250 operational hours, and then when we've done them we've finished our tour of ops and we go home."

"We've got 10 hours to do. By the end of the week, it will be U.K. for us."

"How did you know?" said Aussie.

"Flight Commander, he said you were a very experienced crew."

"Just lucky, more like."

"Shut up Aussie, I've got some letters to write."

"I suppose you're all looking forward to leaving and telling people when to expect you home?" I was not very sensitive to atmosphere, but soon realised that everyone had stopped and was looking at me.

"Have I said something wrong?" I said.

"Don't ever say anything like that again, you silly bastard."

"Now, now," interrupted the navigator, "Why, he hasn't got his knees brown yet." I glanced down and a wave of laughter broke.

"God, you are raw. When someone says your knees are not brown, it means you lack experience. Do you understand that?" There was a pause. "You realise that we are on ops tonight?" I nodded.

"Well, don't worry about it. We'll show you what to do. I suggest you spend the time getting your kit ready. You have got some, I suppose?"

"Yes, it's outside near the guard room. I must go and get it."

"You do that, son."

It was fairly easy to find my way to the flight commander's office and to my relief the baggage was still there; but it was not until I tried to go back that I realised that all the tents looked the same!

Meanwhile, the Flight Commander was doing his best to forget the pale young face of his new pilot. With a sigh, he turned to the unfinished letter on his table.

"Dear Mrs. Pinch," it read, "I am deeply sorry to have to tell you ..."

CHAPTER TWO

# My First Operation

The air crackled with tension as the aircrews entered the
shabby dusty tent that was being used for briefing. As we
filed in, each of us tackled our fear in our own way, some
of us turning within ourselves, walking like zombies, stumbling
over guy-ropes, as with tight lips we thought about our loved
ones at home; others talked incessantly in a loud nervous way,
and yet others laughed raucously over unfunny stories. I was
among them, a boy who had more reason than the others to be
afraid; for it would be my first operation against the enemy. I
could feel the tension in the air as the other aircrews sat, each
occupying their own collapsible bench, waiting for the briefing to
start. Suddenly, as one man, a crew stood up, and the tail-gunner,
sitting at the end, was thrown to the floor as the counterbalancing
weight of his crew members was removed. A gale of laughter
passed through the crowd at this ridiculous childhood prank. Any
weak joke, any prep-school action seemed enough to lighten the
atmosphere.

And yet this all brought back memories to me of a time when I
was once again frightened. It was my first day on the training ship
*Warspite*. We had finished scrubbing the upper deck with bare feet
and cold Thames water and came down to the mess deck for
breakfast. Two boys were told to go to the galley to fetch the meal.
They soon brought back two mess tins and a huge teapot, and so it
wasn't long before we were all tucking in.

A few minutes passed and then there was a crack and three of us
boys found ourselves sprawling on the deck as the bench collapsed

from underneath us. A roar of laughter from the rest of the boys greeted us as, embarrassed, we fixed the bench again.

A hush fell over the audience as a procession of senior officers made their way to the front.

"Any bets it's Tobruk," whispered the wireless op as we all stood up. There was a rustle as half a dozen air-crews balanced their weight once again upon the shaky seats.

I watched with interest as the officers climbed up on to the ramshackle platform made of tables. A little man with the four rings of a group captain waited impatiently for the noise of the platform party to cease, and then he looked at the air-crews who were still chuckling over the discomfort of their tail-gunner. I felt a dislike for this man, who seemed so full of his own importance.

"The programme tonight," he said eventually, "is similar to last night. I've been informed that a heavy build-up of forces is threatening in the Tobruk area, and we must do everything we can to stop it."

There were no smiles or chuckles now. The marquee was silent and still while the distant roar of an engine under test built up to a crescendo before dying away. I could sense the atmosphere, even though I did not know that Tobruk had more defences per square yard than Berlin.

"I know," went on the group captain in his bumptious way, "that some of you took a pasting last night. Well," he shrugged his shoulders, "we must expect it. I think that's all ... Oh no, I nearly forgot: crew of P for Peter should be congratulated, damn fine show ..." All this was over my head, although it did remind me of the Headmaster's assembly at school, when the football team were congratulated by a Head who really did not give a damn.

"No, I'll leave all the details to your Flight Commander. Good luck, chaps, and keep a cool head." He jumped down into the sand and stomped away.

Was it my imagination, or was there really a look of irritation upon the face of the Flight Commander as he moved forward? I watched as he pinned up a strange map drawn upon a grid of concentric circles. The easel was designed to be kept stable by a length of rope, but this had disappeared long ago and so it slowly began to do the splits. He paused, pulled the easel up to its full height and started again.

"We are operating against Tobruk and so the target map is the same as last night. There is only one slight difference. You don't need me to tell you that this target is very hot." He paused and looked around. Was I imagining that his gaze lingered a little in different parts of the tent?

"To make it a little easier, we have organised a blitz period. At 6 minutes past 3 I want all crews to make their run at the same time. This should help, for they cannot concentrate on more than one aircraft at a time. 50 Squadron and 106 will be operating, and as this means that eighteen aircraft will be in the area, a good look-out must be maintained at all times. 125 Squadron will be at 15,000 feet to give you fighter cover."

"Lot of good that will be," grunted the gunner on my left.

"Bombing height will be the usual 6,000, and all aircraft will do one photo run after bombing. Are there any questions?" No one answered, so the Flight Commander continued. "Take-off time, 22:45. All crews to be at readiness and engines tested by 22:13. Order of take-off will be alphabetical: Apple, George, Johnnie, Sugar, X-ray. You have already been assigned to aircraft." He sat down and his place was taken by the tall, bony figure of the Engineering Officer.

"All aircraft," he started, "have been filled with 90% fuel load, which should be plenty for this run. With a 4,000-pound bomb, that should give you a maximum altitude of around 6,500. You have all tested your aircraft. Remember to sign the Form 700 before take-off. Oh, and there is one further point …" He paused and looked at the Flight Commander, who gave a slight nod:

"Can I ask you to stop pissing on the tyres of the aircraft?" Grins appeared everywhere, much to his annoyance. "You may think it is funny, but the urine is having a serious effect upon the rubber. You can remember what happened to B-for-Bertie when a tyre burst on take-off." The audience was hushed. They were only too aware of the hole in the sand, and the ingots of molten aluminium.

The next to appear was the Met officer. Aussie, our wireless op, leaned forward. Holding his hand over his mouth, he attracted my attention.

"Now he'll tell us all about his big toe."

By this time the Met man had pinned up his collection of synoptic charts and was rapidly explaining the weather situation.

"Wind at 6,000 will be 035, 10 knots. All other winds will be available to navigators later. And so, in conclusion, gentlemen, may I remind you that approaching low pressure will cause your altimeters to over-read. Remember stratus cloud is coming in thick from the south and may very well reach here by tomorrow. This, incidentally, is confirmed by my big toe, for today it has begun to ache." There were polite smiles everywhere but most were too wrapped up in their own thoughts to be worried about his big toe.

The last person to speak was the intelligence officer. who explained at length the details of the target, the alterations in the defences and the spine-chilling statistics of the amount of anti-aircraft defence we would encounter.

"To end, may I remind you that in case of an accident always keep your parachute; and above all, make certain that you always have your goolie chit."

As we filed out of the marquee, I kept close behind my captain. "What's a goolie chit?"

"It's a card written in four or five Arabic languages explaining that you are an important member of the forces of the white king across the sea, and that if anything happens to you, then the white king across the sea will have their guts for garters."

"But why is it called a goolie chit?"

"Because natives around here have a nasty habit of cutting off the testicles of any prisoner. They add them to the stew, you know; airman's balls are the main delicacy."

"You're pulling my leg," I said nervously. "Have you known it happen to anyone?"

"Only once, and then the chap was accused of rape. Still if you haven't got one, you'd better see the brains department and they will issue you with one. See you later, and then we'll take the crew-bus together."

The time seemed to drag and the hands of my watch seemed to be quite still during the hours after briefing, but gradually the time went and I joined Frenchie and the two gunners for the pre-flight check. Aussie was away attending a wireless briefing and Roy was hidden away working on his flight plan. I watched as Frenchie checked the Form 700 with the corporal while the gunners loaded their twin Brownings. I strolled underneath the aircraft and studied with interest the great yawning gap in the black plane's stomach. I stood to one side as the ugly great bomb was wheeled into position, and joined Frenchie who was studying a repair that had been done to the Pitot head.

"What's she like aerodynamically when that great hole is open to the slipstream?"

"Not a great deal of difference," said Frenchie, as he moved an aileron to and fro. "She becomes a little nose-heavy perhaps, but when we drop the bomb we lift vertically for about 500 feet."

I noticed that the normal bomb-beam had been removed, and that the seeming collection of oil drums was being winched up by a cable around its centre of gravity. It was a bit crude, I thought, as I watched the armourer winding it into place. I looked up to find Frenchie had climbed into the cockpit, and so I continued my idle tour of inspection by strolling under the front turret. As I looked up, I could see the gunner sitting in his perspex bubble 15 feet above me. I watched as the gunner rotated the barrels of the twin Brownings to test for the full range of movement, and I wondered if it was true that the average life of an air-gunner really was 6 weeks on ops. Certainly these two had lasted longer than that, as they were nearly time-expired. They must be either clever or, as they put it, damn lucky.

We all met again in the dining marquee. Supper was the only good thing of the night. Most of us were not very hungry, and the meal was a quiet, subdued affair. We stayed there having a last cigarette until the crew bus took us to the crew room.

Carefully I emptied my pockets, placing all my personal effects in my locker. I then checked that I had my new goolie chit, and anything else that would be useful if I met the enemy.

Many others did a similar thing, I discovered; why, even Frenchie kept a sheath knife tucked in the top of his sock, probably a souvenir of his life in Canada. The aircraft at readiness were in dispersal bays over a large area and the crew bus was working overtime. Some of the air-crews stood outside having a last cigarette and watching the jeep moving slowly across the airfield, while the controller for the night switched on each individual light for the flare-path.

"It's a job I've always wanted," I overheard, "The one belonging to the chap at home who lights all the red lights around a hole in the road and then sits all night in a hut warming himself with a coke-burning stove."

"Not much future in that." "You think there is in this?"

The speaker dropped his cigarette, stood on it, and walked into the crew-room.

Meanwhile, Roy the navigator had just finished his flight-plan and was checking his equipment. Charts, maps, star tables, Met forecast, two pencils, two dividers, rubber, encoding machine, and sextant were all there. He rammed them all into his hold-all and for a moment looked through the flap of the tent. A flurry of wind whipped up the sand and set the guy-ropes rattling against the canvas. If everything went well we should be back by five in the morning. Sky, he thought, was clear, air stable; there should be no difficulty over astro. Arcturus was ideal for a 90-degree position-line.

However, Tobruk was a target that filled everyone with dread. Rarely did the squadron escape without some casualties. Yet it was easy to ignore it, or to pretend to ignore it. After all, we went off one aircraft at a time and we came back one at a time – or we didn't. There were always these empty places in the mess, always the same excuse, but everyone knew that chalk marks in the control room at Group had recorded the disappearance. Sometimes over the target they would see a Wimp falling earthwards, a plume of flame streaming from the fuselage, but it was best not to think of such things. After all, it would never happen to them. Frenchie was an inspired pilot. He could throw the plane around like a Tiger Moth, and he had an original mind that always came up with something.

Roy's mind wandered to the latest member of the crew. There was something about him that reminded him of home. He was young, and innocent, and with his spotty face he was like so many of his pupils at home. He remembered the old stone buildings of Gray-thorpe Grammar School. Well, he had done his best to keep things going. More and more of the staff were called up until it was inevitable that it would be his turn soon. That was why he had joined the R.A.F. After all, if he had to leave his wife and children, then it was better to volunteer. Forcing himself to face the present, he picked up the bulging hold-all and joined the young novice outside.

"What say to walking out? Our aircraft is only just over there."
As we strolled along, I helped Roy carry his gear.
"Are you frightened?" he enquired. "A bit."
"Don't worry; you'll be all right with us."
The others had walked ahead. When they arrived at the aircraft, it was obvious to me that something was wrong.
"It's all right, Frenchie, for him to say that," moaned Nipper the gunner, "but things won't be the same if we don't."
"That's just a superstition," retorted the Canadian. "You've been the first to remind us in the past." "Tell you what," drawled Aussie, "can't we go through the motions without actually using the wheel?"
"Good idea," said Frenchie, quick to realise the possibility of a compromise, "we'll use the starboard wing. Come on, crew – form a straight line with Nipper outboard."
I had no real idea as to what was going on, but the others were quick to catch on. Nipper walked to the wing-tip, followed in turn by Nipper the front gunner.
"It won't be the same," he grumbled, shaking his head, "it just won't be the same."
"Of course it will," said Roy, throwing the weight of his maturity on to his skipper's argument.
"I'll stand next to you – and Bill, you next. About 2 yards apart should do it."
Slowly the line formed up under the huge wing.
The corporal fitter sat on the starter trolley and watched to see what was going on.
"Right, men," shouted Frenchie, "Atten-tion." The crew jumped to attention as far as their parachutes would allow.
"On the command 'Go,' you release your parachutes."
"One, two, three, *go*."
As one man, they brought their right hands over to snap the quick release buckle.
"One pace forward march. On the command 'two', you will take another step forward. On 'three' you will open your flies, and on 'four', you will present your prick for inspection. Pissing by numbers, begin."

Like airmen on parade they shouted, "One, pause two, pause three, pause four." Timing their actions as Frenchie had instructed.

"Good men, good, now piss."

I found I could urinate as well as the others. Perhaps it was the tension.

Meanwhile the corporal sat on the trolley grinning. Still, he'd seen this sort of ritual before. If they thought it helped, then good luck to them. *Rather them than me*, he reflected, thinking of his drinks in the N.A.A.F.I...

"O.K. men, chutes on," ordered Frenchie, "Its time we were aboard."

As second pilot, I was the last to enter the plane. I watched as, one by one, they climbed up the five aluminium rungs to disappear into the bowels of the aircraft. I knew exactly what I would discover. I knew that the ladder went up through the floor into the cockpit, and that if I were to walk toward the tail, then I would pass the navigator's table and the wireless op's chair. Poor Aussie, he had to face forward with his head only inches from the brightly coloured knobs of his radio. Going further aft meant clambering over the main beam that took the weight of the wings, and entering rather an empty section with a camp bed, a chemical toilet, and a chute for photoflashes. There was a window on either side here which at one time, I believed, had been used for gun positions. Now, with the geodetic construction breaking up the perspex into diamond panes, it gave the place an almost arty-crafty look.

The front gunner, I knew, would have to crawl forward, while the captain and I would sit at the controls above the entrance hatch, which when closed formed part of the bomb-aimer's position.

I followed Frenchie up the ladder. Why did all aeroplanes smell the same? It was an odd smell of oil and plastic that was common to every aircraft in the world. Carefully I pulled up the ladder and closed the hatch. Now we were ready to start.

From where I was sitting I could see over the starboard wing, with the round cowl of the Pegasus engine jutting out from the leading edge. I gazed across at the other Wimpies, their propellers beginning to move in a staccato fashion, as each cylinder went into compression at top dead centre.

Frenchie had his oxygen mask unclipped at the side and was shouting through the window at the corporal below.

"Brakes on, switches off," he shouted, starting the usual litany of procedure.

"Contact," he cried, as he pressed the starter button with one hand and flicking up the two ignition switches with the other, making the engine roar into life.

"Contact starboard," he repeated and soon the propeller on my side became a blur of movement. The corporal unhitched the starter cable and moved it to a safe distance while the Wimp's engines ticked over, until the oil temperature and pressure seemed correct.

Then there came the chance to escape. Roy and Aussie looked over my shoulder at the trembling instruments. Would there be a big rev drop at this last moment? If there was, then the operation would be cancelled and we could sleep safely in our beds for another night.

Frenchie leaned forward, adjusted the throttle friction nut and carefully increased the revs of the port engine. I knew that each engine had two ignition systems complete with their own sets of sparking plugs, and each set controlled by its own ignition switch. The needle of the rev counter moved upward and the roar of the engine increased. At 1,000 revs, Frenchie took his hand from the throttle and reached for the ignition switches. Who would not run away if a chance was given? Frenchie operated one switch: there was no drop in revs, so he switched it back on and then tried the other. The engine still roared away as if nothing had happened. Quietly, he throttled back and repeated with the other engine. The others lost interest, and returned to their stations while Frenchie the captain clipped on his mask, switched on the R.T., and called Control.

"Hello Caesar, hello Caesar, S-for-Sugar ready and clear to taxi from dispersal? Over."

"Hello, Sugar – you may taxi to Control. Direction of take-off 32, Q.F.E. 004. Over."

"Hello Caesar, S-for-Sugar, wilco, over and out."

He switched back to intercom.

"O.K. you shower, we're on our way."

He waved the chocks away and glanced to right and left. The corporal was right ahead by this time, and by following his instructions the Wimp slowly swung round to point its nose at the black-and-white chequered control hut parked on the perimeter.

We bumped our way over the sand as the other aircraft took off in a steady stream.

"Flash S for Sugar on the downward indent," ordered Frenchie. I leaned forward and tapped the three flashes.

I had always been fascinated by flare-paths. They seemed to go on, and on, to the very horizon, where lines of lights slowly converged with perspective. I turned my attention to Frenchie, who was doing his pre-flight check. Pitch, flaps, throttle control nut, direction indicator on nought, and brakes hard on. Slowly but surely he opened both throttles until the whole plane shook and vibrated as the roaring engines strained against the locked-on brakes.

"Here we go boys, say goodbye to Leicester Square." He released the brakes, and the plane jumped forward like a carthorse released from its shafts. I hoped it wouldn't develop the simile too closely by suddenly rolling over. Soon we were bouncing over the ruts as the lights of the flare-path began to fly by.

I am sure we were all scared. The moment of takeoff, particularly with a 4,000-pounder, was fraught with danger. I clenched my hands until my knuckles were white as the plane seemed to take over with a life of its own. The tail was up and there was that strange unstable feel, when suddenly there was a roar and everything disappeared in fog. Many times I had taken off in my short career, but never before had I lost visibility at 90 mph. It was like racing at night with no brakes, and then hitting a bank of fog. All sense of direction left me. Were we on the flare-path, and above all did we have enough speed to become airborne? In a flash, I remembered the post-man saying that once we took off with that sort of bomb there was no turning back. I sat frozen with horror.

As suddenly as it had fogged, so the visibility returned, the vibration ceased and Frenchie, hiding his relief, leaned forward and selected "Undercarriage Up". As in a nightmare, I watched the little green lights turn to red as the wheels came up to lock in the fuselage.

"What the hell happened?" cried Aussie.

Frenchie looked at me and pointed downwards. I looked down between my legs and was astonished to see the lights of the outer circle shining through a hole. There was nothing but five hundred feet of air between my seat and the darkened landscape.

"You didn't close the hatch properly; you could have killed us all you silly bastard. Better get down and shut it and make certain it's properly closed or we may fall out." My face red with shame, I unstrapped myself and carefully closed the hatch. When I finally plugged in again to the intercom I heard the cries of protest from the rest of the crew. I looked around and noticed that the throttle assembly was covered in fine yellow sand. Had I looked behind me I would have seen Roy emptying the sand from his charts and books, while Aussie was blowing it from beneath his morse key.

Later that night, while I was sitting in the captain's seat concentrating upon my direction indicator, the compass and the artificial horizon, I had time to think. To think that carelessness upon my part had brought us to the brink of disaster, saved only by the experience of Frenchie who could lift the aircraft off blindfold, and by feel alone. I glanced at the muffled figure to my left and wondered whether I too would soon be like that.

## CHAPTER THREE

# Over the Target

W e climbed steadily away on course and things in the plane settled down to routine. A 60-degree dog-leg enabled Roy to establish a wind, while the gunners kept ceaseless watch for enemy attack. There was not much chance of that as, for once, the Allies had achieved air superiority. Nevertheless, to be on the safe side, Aussie was listening out trying to assess fighter activity by the amount of German RIT.

"Navigator to Skipper," squeaked the intercom, "level out at 5,000 feet, airspeed one, eight, zero."

"Wilco."

"Met winds are spot on tonight, E.T.A. target 3:13."

"Well done," replied Frenchie, "I'm handing over to Bill now while I get some rest. Have you got the target map? I want to have a gander at it."

I stood up and collapsed my seat against the wall.

Frenchie gave me a thumbs-up and then released his safety harness. It was a bit of a job, changing seats, but Frenchie had adjusted the trim very well and I discovered that just a gentle pressure on the stick was enough as my captain sidled out of the way. It was then Frenchie's turn to hold the controls as I made myself comfortable in the seat with my harness tightly on. It only took a few minutes and then I felt at home again, indeed I felt proud to be flying. The controls seemed a little heavy until I realised that it needed a little nosetrim to compensate for Frenchie's walking aft. I bent down and moved the trimming wheel and immediately the controls became light as the trimming tabs moved down into the slipstream, forcing the elevators up. I must remember that trim, I thought. After all, when properly balanced the plane would fly itself; it was foolish to make it hard work.

My eyes wandered over the instrument panel, for I was determined not to make a mistake again. I looked down at the compass. Yes, the grid ring was clamped properly on course, and the compass needle was lying in the middle of the wires. And yet I was not completely happy, for the wires and compass needle were not absolutely parallel. Carefully I banked the plane a few degrees to the left. The direction indicator moved from 268 to 290. I concentrated on keeping the plane straight for a few minutes before glancing again at the compass. That was better, the needle and wires were all lined up. It was the fault of the direction indicator, it must have gone wrong. It was the work of a minute to adjust it to 285; and soon I had settled back, keeping the plane a few degrees on either side of course.

Sitting in the dark with the only light a green ghostly glow from the instruments, I remembered long ago when I was a seaman at the wheel in the middle watch. The gyro compass was the same as the D.I., with a tendency to send one to sleep. I smiled to myself as I remembered that at the time the crew were always eating toffees. Now we were all chewing too, but this time it was gum issued to help alleviate the tension.

When at sea, the crew had called upon me to do a little job. It seemed that in the hold were two large tanks. They knew that the empty space in the tanks would be sublet for something else, and so "the boy" – me – had to go down and check them over. One was full of loose toffees, and so we all helped ourselves for the rest of the voyage. This mystified the Mate, because he kept finding toffee papers on the deck. His problem was that the space in the tanks did not appear on the manifest, so he had no idea they were there.

I sat there watching the little model aircraft on the display of the artificial horizon, keeping it steady, not up or down, with both little wings in line with the straight line drawn on the instrument. I relied on that, although I thought some people like Frenchie could fly by the seat of their pants.

I glanced at my instruments and noticed that I had carelessly allowed the nose to drop and so the air-speed was increasing. I must be careful, or Roy would be after me for that. But it was not my fault this time, for the trim had altered as Frenchie came back into the cockpit.

"I'll take over now," he said, "we're getting close to E.T.A."

The usual business of changing seats began, and soon I could stand and stretch my legs that were stiff after my turn at the controls.

"Captain to crew," called Frenchie, "we're getting close to the target, so be on your guard. Nipper, keep a close look-out on the ground will you, there are a number of army units around here and we only need one shell."

"O.K. Skipper, haven't seen anything so far."

"Nipper," interrupted Roy, "keep an eye open for that destroyer that we were told about at briefing."

"O.K. Wilco."

I looked out to starboard, where I could see the coast with its leaden sea. I tried to remember the target map in order to discover how far we had to go. It wouldn't be long now, and so a wave of fear swept over me. Suddenly I felt very cold.

"Searchlights ahead, Skipper," sounded the excited voice of Nipper.

"O.K. I've got them." "Could that be the target?"

Roy left his chart-table and peered through the windscreen.

"Yes, that's it right enough."

"O.K. then, I'll work my way around to the left and do a few circuits before we go in."

"What about the I.F.F.?" called Roy.

"Yes, good idea," replied the Captain. "Listen, Aussie, when we're over the target I want you to be ready to switch it on and off every two seconds. I'll let you know when to start."

There was a rumour that this rapid switching affected the enemy radar, and so the searchlights; and Frenchie was not the sort of person to ignore a thing like that.

Looking out, I was surprised to see how beautiful it was. This was the last adjective I would have expected to use, yet nonetheless it was true. The moon, larger and bigger than in England, was half hidden by a long streaming wisp of cloud, while the long yellow fingers from the searchlights waved ceaselessly backwards and forwards, continuously searching like the poisonous delicate feelers of a gigantic sea anemone sifting the water for its prey.

Every now and again they would switch and lock into a rigid pyramid, and then I would see a minute silver aircraft turning and twisting like a fly caught in a spider's web. Then from everywhere would appear a curtain of graceful dotted lines in green and gold and crimson, which curved up in splendid parabolas of light, to form a sparkling arch of fire about 1,000 feet below. The night sky was full of sudden flashes, and I happened to be looking at the right place for one to burst, directly in my vision, when I saw a yellow flash with a sudden red centre, like a monstrous sunflower. And yet it was all so silent, like a clip from a silent colour movie, for with our flying helmets and the monotonous drone of the engines all other sounds were blotted out.

"Well, there's no use waiting," called Frenchie, "let's get it over and done with. Roy, set the bombsight for 6,000 feet, air speed 150."

"O.K. Skipper."

Roy left his chart-table and crawled between my legs, where he laid on his stomach looking down at the target below.

"Ready, Skipper," he shouted, and I watched as he armed the bomb, and grasped the bomb-release switch with a gloved hand.

"Here we go, chaps – hold tight!"

Frenchie turned the aircraft on to a course that would bring us over the 1,000 anti-aircraft guns. Almost immediately we were illuminated as if we were on the stage.

Frenchie swung the aircraft over in a 90-degree bank and pulled hard back on the stick to tighten the turn, then with a hard push on his bottom leg he pressed hard on the rudder. The Wimp vibrated as she approached a stall; then, tipping over on one wingtip, spun round and pivoted, until she was plunging towards earth in a vertical dive.

Automatically Frenchie had assessed the underreading of the altimeter and had decided to pull out at 3,500 feet. Gritting his teeth, he sat motionless at the controls while I am sure every fibre in his body was calling out to him to stop this headlong dive. I watched as the air-speed indicator moved relentlessly towards the red sector and the altimeter hands spun round in a crazy fashion like a clock that had lost the constraints of its escapement. As the finger of the altimeter rotated quickly round from 4,000 to 3,000, Frenchie pulled hard back on the stick. As he had expected, the controls were locked solid by the tremendous power of the howling slipstream.

Muscles, hardened by years of labour on the land in Canada, tensed, as with all his strength he heaved as he had never heaved before. Slowly the nose came up; we all felt tightness in our faces, a red curtain dropped over our eyes, and for a moment the plane flew itself. When we had recovered, the plane was beginning to climb.

I was standing by my captain's side. Instinctively I had shaded my eyes from the searchlight's glare. I concentrated upon the blind flying panel as Frenchie fought the controls. To my horror all the gyro controlled instruments toppled, becoming useless. In desperation I looked up to orientate myself, but there was nothing to see but lights that had somehow left the safe anchorage of the ground, gyrating in all directions, so that at times the blazing target seemed to be above us. Sometimes I felt strangely light and then weight would pile upon me like a giant hand, relentlessly forcing me to the floor. My legs could stand it no longer, and I collapsed across the feet of the prostrate bomb-aimer.

*This is it*, I thought, *this is it* … but as soon as I had collapsed, the giant hand relaxed and my dizziness cleared. I pulled myself together and studied the instrument panel again. I could hardly believe my eyes, for the air-speed was 280 – but, thank goodness, dropping – while the altimeter was reading only 1,500 feet. The plane shot out to sea as Nipper complained, "Christ! – you nearly gave me wet feet."

"Sorry," said Frenchie as we roared over the waves, "I hope you haven't too many bruises."

"You were a bit drastic," shouted Aussie "I thought I was going through the set."

"Yeah, well I blacked out too, still we'd better climb up to six thou and have another go."

I was trembling with fear: was this what bombing operations were like? Never had I seen a bomber aircraft thrown about like this before. Of all the crew, I knew how near we had been to disaster and yet they were now calmly saying that they were going to do it again. I closed my eyes and prayed.

"Please God," I thought, "don't let us do it again." We circled in comparative safety as we gained height for a new run. The intercom crackled as Nipper's voice came over.

"Gunner to Captain," he shouted, "there's an aircraft over there with a light on."

"Yes, I can see it; it's at 10 o'clock about 3,000 feet above us." I moved to one side as Aussie and Roy joined me in the cockpit.

"He's not going over the target like that, is he?" "Poor bastard probably doesn't know it's on."

We watched, fascinated, as the speck of light circled the town.

"Can't we get him on R/T or something?" "No he's on a different frequency."

Suddenly the speck altered course and approached the target. All the searchlights went out and left the red glows of the fires to mark the town. In the deadly pause the light continued, with its pilot probably puzzled at his lucky reprieve. Then it happened: with every searchlight locking on to the unfortunate aircraft, I could see it wriggling like a butterfly with a needle in its head as the gunners filled the sky with metal from their gunnery practice.

"It's a Halifax," shouted Nipper, and then we all cheered as the searchlights began weaving again.

"He's got away, can you see him Nipper?"

"Yes there, he is, to port."

"Get back to your places, you two," said Frenchie, quickly. "I've got an idea. Next time that poor so-and-so goes in, we go in too."

"Can you hear me Roy?" "Loud and clear, Skipper."

"Set the sight for 4,000 feet and 200 mph." "Did you say 4,000?" Roy queried.

"Yes, that heavy flak has been fused for 5,000 and it'll take them time to adjust the fuses."

"And 200 mph?"

"Yes, you'll have to be nippy. I'm going to dive down and bring the nose up at the last minute."

"Skipper," called Nipper, "that light stuff is coning at 5,000."

"Sure thing, they probably know that we have been told to bomb from there. Don't worry; we can fly through that stuff without damage."

I stood gripping the nearest geodetic until my knuckles were white.

"He's going in, Capt."

"Right – stand by, boys, here we go."

The aircraft banked to the left until it took up its new course.

"Going down."

I watched as Frenchie cut his throttles and began to dive. I could now look forward and see the ground with all its fires and flashes. I swallowed quickly as the change in pressure made me deaf while the dotted streams of tracer came closer and closer, and then we were through and the fountain of light was above us. Frenchie heaved once again on the stick.

"Left, left," shouted Roy, "steady ... *right* a little."

He drawled the word in contrast to the staccato 'left'.

"210," shouted Frenchie, "205 and falling." "Left. left, air speed steady."

"200 and steady."

I knew that Frenchie was working hard to keep the aircraft straight and level. Suddenly I felt my legs become weak as the aircraft rose like a lift.

"Bomb gone."

Frenchie wrenched the aircraft round again in another steep turn, opening the throttles at the same time. As if eager to return home, the plane twisted round and left the target. The job was done. It was only then that I realised the strain that I had been through. And then I saw Frenchie looking at me.

"Did you say something?" I asked.

"Yeah, I said are you ready to work on the photoflash?"

They were going to do it again, and this time I would have to take my share!

It appeared to me that warfare had a strange remoteness about it, seeming to be just technician pitted against technician. I and my comrades had been trained to use our technology for maximum results, to make a calculated assessment of stresses and strains. If we managed to get the sums right, if we behaved as we had been trained to do, then the 4,000-pound bomb would drop just where we had planned. On the other hand, the radar operators and gun-layers below were behaving in a similar clinical manner. They too were working against time, making split-second decisions. If they were successful, then a silver bird fluttered down from the sky; and they were thrilled at their success, marred in no way by thoughts of injuries and death to the crew. Both sides were pitting their skills and training against each other, and to me it was only the actions of the defenders that changed it into a terrifying nightmare of apprehension.

Of course my crew had no idea whether we had succeeded. The bomb had fallen into the welter of flame, flashes, and smoke. Whether it had fallen innocently into the desert sands or had turned railroads, hospitals and schools into acres of crumbling masonry inhabited by blood-covered victims with missing limbs could only be told by a careful analysis of photographs. Frenchie and the others had done it many times before, but to me it was a shock to know that we had to fly over the target again, and that this time I had to play my part in making the technology work. For the first time the lives of my friends would be dependent upon my actions.

I knew that strapped to the side of the aircraft were three metal tubes painted red, with "DANGER" stencilled in black along their length. They were 3 feet long and about 6 inches in diameter, and I knew they were filled with a nasty mixture of magnesium powder and phosphorus.

When I had sat bored through the endless lectures by the corporal "armaments", I had not realised the importance of the message.

"Five million candle power, that's how bright a photoflash is, and if it goes off in your hands it will make Guy Fawkes night look like a kindergarten."

At O.T.U. they had a mock-up of a Wimpy's fuselage. One at a time, we had climbed the steps into the aluminium framework. We were shown how to push out the flare-chute until it extended 3 feet outside the aircraft. In my mind I could remember the Cockney corporal's words:

"There are two safety devices on a photoflash. The first is this horseshoe-shaped retainer. It fits over the screw of the tail-fin. That fin, you see, must rotate fifty times before it spins off, and it should happen after the flash has fallen 100 feet below the plane. Then, *bzoom!* – up it goes, blasting everything within about 50 feet. So it's safe as long as the retainer is on ... Unless," he grinned, "some red-hot flak hits it while you are giving it a cuddle."

I had been keen on fishing, and my mind had wandered a bit while I was being shown the fishing reel and line attached to the aircraft roof. It seemed that one had to pull out the line, attach it to the horse-shoe retainer and give the flare a shove. It then fell, pulling out the wire, and only when its 20 feet had been unreeled did the jerk whip out the retainer, allowing the tail-fin to spin.

As in a dream, I heard Frenchie urging me to get a move on. With a stomach like lead, I clipped my parachute pack on to my chest, unplugged the intercom, and made my way into the dark interior. I noticed the dull blue light shining over the navigator's chart as I squeezed past the empty seat, for Roy was still in the bomb-aimer's position. In the dark I stumbled over the navigator's bag that had been left in the gangway. Picking myself up, I felt along the wall for the lethal containers. They should be opposite the radio position; but there was no comparison between this and my dry run at O.T.U.

As Frenchie dodged and jinked, I was thrown about like a dry pea in a drum. With feet far apart, and holding on with one hand, I wrestled with the stiff canvas retaining strap; but even this was difficult. I had to force open the catch by feel alone, and with my parachute on my chest and the violent movement of the plane, it just would not come free. And all the time I knew that Frenchie and the rest of the crew were fuming because I was so slow. I was not plugged in to the intercom, and so was alone in a world of my own. In desperation, I wrenched at the stiffened strap. At the same time a sudden drop added strength to my pull, the catch gave way and the cylinder fell forward into my arms. Thank God it had come free. Now I must hurry to get it ready for launching. I fell rather than stepped over the main beam into the launching area, stumbling as the plane jinked. I felt disorientated: feeling along the geodetics, I was relieved to find the round entrance to the flare-chute. I reclaimed my balance and quickly rammed the flare into the chute.

Now for the fishing line … It was so dark that I had to run my hands over the ceiling of the fuselage. Ah, there it was… and although the wire seemed strangely stiff, soon it was attached to the little copper loop of the retainer. Now for the intercom. I felt around for the sausage-shaped jack, plugged in, and reported that everything was ready.

"And about time too. O.K. then, we'll go in now.

Roy will tell you exactly when to launch. By the way, Bill, hold on really tight because we've got to get away afterwards." I didn't need telling, for I was black and blue all over as it was. I felt the aircraft bank to port and then level out on the new course.

"Stand by, Bill" came over, faint, in the earphones. "We're going over the target now."

I gripped hard to the top of the photoflash. I longed to see out, to see the flashes and the flak; somehow it seemed ten times worse to be shut in that black cage of canvas and aluminium. It was like being down a mine and waiting for an explosion. I closed my eyes and forced myself to concentrate on that armament lecture of months ago. *If it goes off in your hands it will make Guy Fawkes night look like a kindergarten.*

Why couldn't I get that out of my mind?

"Can you hear me, Bill?" Roy's voice brought me back to reality.

"Loud and clear."

"I'll count you down. Here we go, five, four, three, two, one, *now*." Gripping the flash with both hands, I pushed with all my might. The flare was jammed. In desperation I pushed and pushed, but it was stuck fast.

"It's stuck, I can't move it, it won't move either way." A burst of profanity greeted me.

"All right, we'll just have to escape until it's free."

Aussie, you'd better go back and see what's happened. We can't have a flash stuck halfway out of the plane." My face burned with shame, as it was the one thing for which I was responsible, and I'd let them down. But was it my fault? In desperation, I unclipped my parachute to give myself more room to move, but there was no doubt the flare was well and truly jammed. A touch on my shoulder and Aussie was beside me. What was he trying to say? He was making actions at the intercom and then at his helmet. Suddenly it dawned on me that there was only one intercom position. I watched as Aussie unplugged the jack and plugged in his own. Obviously he was using the intercom to talk to the others, but what he was saying was a closed book to me as I was now unplugged.

Aussie came up to me and fumbled with his helmet. It dawned on me that he was going to talk to me. I unbuttoned my helmet and flinched as the sudden roar of the engines bombarded my eardrums. Aussie placed his mouth close to my ear.

"The loo," he shouted, "the loo."

By this time I was in torture. The roar of the engines, the violent actions of the plane, the darkness, my helplessness, my invisible tears of shame … and now I couldn't even understand English! Aussie tried again.

"The lavatory, you've jammed it in the lavatory.

The chute is on the other side. Grab it round the top and I'll help you at the bottom, and we'll pull it free."

I then realised what I had done. The chemical closet was directly opposite the chute and in the dark I had mistaken the seat for the chute opening. Together we pulled and wrenched. Without my parachute I could get more purchase, and soon the flare was out, its end wet and dripping, with the seat stuck round its middle like a giant plastic washer. Aussie gave the seat a kick and it snapped off in two pieces. I could just make out Aussie's actions as he pushed out the chute extension and carefully lowered the wet flare into place. He unplugged his intercom and motioned that I should plug mine in.

"Can you hear me, Bill?" called Frenchie.

"I want you to plug in at the navigator's position and leave that socket for Aussie. Do you understand?"

"Yes, but I'm terribly sorry about all this."

"Never mind, it'll make a good yarn when we get back to the mess." I plugged in as requested and discovered a general discussion about what to do now. Aussie seemed to be leading the argument.

"It's all very well, but this is our goddamn last trip. If we go over the target again, we may be blasted into kingdom come."

"Maybe," said Frenchie," but we've got to take a photograph."

"To hell with the photograph, let's dump it over the side and forget it."

"We can't do that, the camera is open all the time and we'll just take a picture of empty desert."

"Can't we drop it without letting it off; pretend it was U/S or something?"

"How about it, Roy?"

"Can't see how we can, Skipper. You see, I have to hand in the horse-shoe retainer to show it's released."

"Say, Roy," interrupted Nipper, "You can fix it."

"Suppose you bend the fins of the propeller so that they can't spin round? It wouldn't work then."

There was a moment's pause.

"Hello, Skipper," – it was Aussie: "I've had a go, and I think I could bend it as Nipper suggested."

"Right, Skipper to all crew, remember if we sabotage this there must be no mention at debriefing. Is that understood?"

A chorus of voices showed that we agreed completely.

"All right, Aussie, let the blasted thing go. Come on, Bill, come back to the cockpit and we'll head for home."

I was just in time to hear Aussie say that the launch was successful. Everybody tried to talk at once.

"I'll tell you this," called Nipper "after that first go over the target, that bog would have been very useful to me. Had I made it then, there would have been no need to fix the flare. It would have needed drying out. E.T.A, in a few minutes."

Everyone laughed, the relief was tremendous. "Navigator to Skipper, course for base 085, I will give you a more accurate course in a minute."

## CHAPTER FOUR

# Disaster Strikes

It seemed strangely peaceful to fly on a steady course after the hectic life over the target. Once again the horizon seemed where it ought to it be, the moon was where it always was, the blind flying instruments were functioning well and the engines hummed along, the blue exhausts flickering along the engine nacelles.

"Roy to Frenchie, E.T.A. base 04:23. But we still have a problem. Perhaps Aussie could give it a little thought?"

"What's wrong, Roy?"

"It's the loo seat. It's broken into two pieces. How do we explain that?"

Frenchie laughed. "You've been putting on a bit of weight, Roy. We'll have to blame you."

There was a natural tendency to relax when leaving the target. Night fighters were rare in the Western Desert.

"Home James, and don't spare the horses," called out Napper.

"Concentrate on your look-out," retorted Frenchie, "We're not home yet."

"Napper," called Nipper, "Do you realise we are finished?"

"Sure thing, it's the U.K. for us in the morning."

"Just think of that poor bastard Bill, he's got a whole tour to do."

"Put a sock in it," called Frenchie, "and Napper keep your eyes skinned, there's no relaxation until we get back."

"Aye, aye, Capt."

I listened in silence. I knew that there was only a one in three chance of completing my tour, but at the moment I didn't seem to care. There was no doubt that Nipper would take great delight in telling the story of the photoflash. Soon I would be the laughing-stock of the squadron. Any minute now, Frenchie would ask me to take over; and then what idiot thing would I do?

And then it happened. Deep down in the darkened desert was a lonely ack-ack gun with a bored gunner with an itchy trigger finger. What chance had he of hitting a passing aircraft? Still, it broke the monotony, and you never know; and so there was a flash and a crack that I could hear over the engine noise and through the protecting ear-muffs of my helmet. I was conscious of a strong smell like fireworks on a damp November evening.

"Christ, we've been hit!" yelled Frenchie through the intercom. I watched anxiously as Frenchie carefully moved the controls in every direction.

"Plane seems O.K."

He turned to me, his face impassive behind its oxygen mask.

"Go back and see what's happened to Roy and Aussie."

I unplugged myself from the intercom, levered myself out of my seat and turned to leave the cockpit. Instantly my eyes took in a scene of utter carnage. The shell had passed through the bombhole in the fuselage to explode inside the aircraft a few feet from Roy and Aussie. The shrapnel had scattered, cutting like a scythe through the flesh of the two now-dead airmen, and had passed through the geodetics of the fuselage, causing little damage apart from rips in the fabric which flapped about in the slipstream like ugly satanic washing. There was blood everywhere. My mind went back to the time when, aged 7, I'd crept through the fence of the local abattoir. I had seen a pit, black and shining from congealed blood, and standing up to his waist in this slimy pit was a man in black sou'wester and oilskins, with a stiff leather holster full of assorted knives. I could remember his tobacco-stained teeth as with a flourish he brandished a knife.

The wireless position was just the same. The radio dripped with blood and Aussie's body sat there, strapped in, and decapitated.

Poor Roy was dead too. Shrapnel had ripped its way up the navigator's left side leaving him a mass of white sinew, shattered bone, and bloody entrails. He had slumped forward on the chart-table where the astrograph projected shadows of equal altitude curves in a pattern upon his still head.

Impossible to control my stomach, I bent over and vomited, my vomit mixing with the blood on the slippery floor. No longer was war an intellectual exercise: it had suddenly become an obscene reality.

A pair of dividers slid to the floor and a red light flashed in my subconscious. The engines were howling as we sped downwards. We were diving. Something must be wrong.

Slipping and sliding, I almost fell back into the cockpit, for by now the angle was extreme. Frenchie had fallen forward, unconscious, pushing the control column forward with the weight of his body. I grabbed the stick and pulled with all my strength, but the speed had built up with the dive and the increased slipstream over the elevators made the control heavy and rigid. Panic gave me renewed strength and as the adrenalin pumped into my body I slowly managed to overcome Frenchie's dead weight to bring the plane back on an even keel.

It was easier then to keep Frenchie away from the controls. His head was slumped forward, and as I shook him I noticed the little jagged hole in the back of the seat where a piece of metal had ripped through, missing the armour-plated pad by a fraction of an inch. There was nothing for it but to fly the plane myself. And it was only then that I realised that my intercom was not plugged in, so holding the control column with one hand I fiddled the jack into the pilot's socket.

"What's wrong, won't anyone tell me?"

I heard with relief the panicky voice of Nipper, the front gunner.

"Yes, it's me, Bill, we've been hit amidships."

"What's the damage?"

"Aussie and Roy have bought it, and now Frenchie has passed out. Can you come back and help me?"

"Sure thing."

I fumbled with the quick-release pin of Frenchie's harness until the body slumped forward as the straps sprung apart. Nipper pushed it forward, and together we pulled him out of the seat as the plane rollercoasted along with its controls sawing backwards and forwards.

I edged into the pilot's seat, while out of the corner of my eye I could see Nipper laying poor Frenchie down in the bomb-aimer's position.

"Skipper's dead," said Nipper quietly, "Are you sure the others have had it?"

Was I sure? – My stomach gave a retch as I remembered. I forced myself to be rational. Would Nipper notice the trembling in my voice?

"I don't know about the tail-gunner, he is not answering the intercom."

"Can you fly the plane O.K.?"

"Yes, the controls are working, there seems to be no trouble there."

Nipper looked at me as if trying to sum up the stranger upon whom all of a sudden his very life depended.

"Good – then I'll go back and see what's happened to Napper."

I forced myself to concentrate on my flying, to try and blot out the memory of the scene behind. Carefully I adjusted the trim until she was flying well and I could afford to take my hands from the controls to strap myself in. After all, one never knew.

"Nipper to Bill, can you hear me?"

"Yes."

"Napper is O.K., at least I think so. It's difficult to make contact because the intercom wires have been cut."

"Can't you get him out of the turret?"

"No, the escape doors have been jammed by a distorted beam and it'll need a damn hacksaw to get him out. Still, he's bashing on the doors, so he is at least alive. I reckon that because the damage was forward of the main spar, he was a long way away from the blast."

"Right, then you had better come forward and we'll decide what to do."

I went over the position in my mind. Skipper, navigator and wireless op dead. I was on my own, and I would have to make the decisions. It seemed obvious to me that I couldn't both navigate and fly the plane. I remembered the map of the Mediterranean in my atlas at school. If I flew due east I should be all right, and the valley of the Nile should stop me from flying too far. Thank God we had plenty of fuel. I flew doggedly on, concentrating upon my flying, but all the time I knew that behind me Nipper was doing his best to clean up the aircraft. He was older than me and had seen death before. I could see him ripping open a parachute and draping the soft white silk over his old friends. One thing was for sure, and that was that they wouldn't need a parachute any longer and it was the least he could do.

But suddenly my mind was forced into the present as the plane yawed violently to the right and a heterodyne beat from the engines made me look left anxiously. I glanced back quickly at the rev counter. My worst fears were realised, for the starboard counter was moving up and down around 300 revs instead of the normal 1,000. Instinctively I moved the throttle forward, and with relief watched the arrow creep up again until the beat of unequal engines disappeared and the revs were the same on both sides. The starboard engine was now running at plus-one boost, and a more experienced pilot would have realised that I had serious trouble; but I was happy that the plane was flying. I failed to realise that this meant engine trouble, increased petrol consumption and very high engine temperatures. By this time Nipper had joined me and was watching the engine anxiously, and so was the person who first saw the glow inside the engine cowling.

"Look," he yelled, "the engine's on fire."

I glanced across the wing in horror as flames whipped from between the cooling fins. Quickly I throttled back while at the same time pushing with all my weight upon the rudder. With the port engine pulling away and the starboard engine dead, it required all my strength to keep the plane on a more or less straight course.

"Can't you stop the fire?"

Fool, why hadn't I thought about that? Feather the prop and switch on the graviner, that was the drill. Graviners were fire extinguishers inside each engine for just such an emergency. I pushed the starboard pitch lever to "feather", and then lifting the spring-loaded cover I pressed the button and watched as a cloud of white vapour streamed across the wing.

"You've done it," shouted Nipper, "you've done it!" But I knew I still had problems, for I had found it necessary to increase the power of the port engine and my leg was throbbing with the strain. Any slight relaxation of the pressure caused a swing off course. There was a trimming tab on the rudder, but even by winding it as far as it would go, it still needed tremendous strength.

"You're not flying straight," said Nipper. "I can see by the direction of the moon."

"I'm doing my best – it's just that the port engine needs full power to stop us losing height."

"Well, we can't stop up here going round in circles until all the gas has gone."

I thought. "Perhaps we should bale out?"

"No chance, you can forget that with Napper stuck in his turret – no, we've got to get this crate onto the ground."

Of course, I thought, Nipper was right; but I was in charge, why couldn't I give the orders? I pondered for a minute, then came to my decision.

"I've got to reduce the power on the port engine. I just can't keep a straight course as it is."

"Does that mean we shall lose height?"

"Yes, we'll just have to stay up as long as possible and then make a crash landing in the desert".

"How long can we keep it up?"

"It depends upon our rate of descent. Here goes." I cautiously moved the throttle lever; it was surprising how just a little reduction in power affected the pressure on my leg.

"That's it, Nipper, look: it's about 100 feet a minute."

On the rate-of-climb indicator it seemed an insignificant amount, but I knew that in under an hour we would be on the ground.

I was astonished to find how normal things were.

The sky was getting lighter away to my left, so it might be light enough to help with the crash landing. My heart gave a lurch as I thought of that, and so I looked down to where I could just make out the bank of cloud about 3,000 feet below. I would have to descend through that, I knew, but it shouldn't give me too much trouble.

I'd wedged my leg in such a way as to take off some of the pressure, and now with the port engine throttled back it was not too uncomfortable. Apart from the starboard rev counter being still, the instruments were all functioning normally. And then I noticed the compass. The needle was not lying along the grid-wires but was 90 degrees to it; we were flying south, and for how long I did not know. Somehow, when we had rotated round with our one engine, we had settled on the wrong course. Slowly, by using every ounce of muscle left in my tired leg, I gradually brought the plane round to its proper direction. But where were we now? Perhaps 100 miles to the south?

No sooner had I swung the aircraft round than I became conscious of the rising mass of cloud. We were so close now that the speed of the bomber was noticeable. In earlier days I had enjoyed spinning along in and out of towering cumulus, but now I was only too aware that I lacked the power for such manoeuvres. I watched it anxiously as it came ever closer, for 100 feet a minute suddenly appeared great; one minute I was whipping just above them, and the next minute sinking deep into the cotton wool ... and then, slap, I was in the featureless fog of the cloudbank and flying completely blind. I had had plenty of training in blind flying, and so it held no terrors for me. All I had to do was concentrate on my instruments until such time as we came out underneath. I noticed that the altimeter was reading 3,000 feet, and so I figured that the cloud was about 1,000 feet thick. This would mean that I would have around 10 minutes of blind flying, followed by another 20 to find a suitable landing place.

It was unfortunate that I had forgotten that at briefing we had been warned of the approaching low pressure area that would cause the altimeter to overread.

Perhaps it was lucky that I did not know that the cloud was down to the ground.

Suddenly there was a flash of white light. Wellington bomber S-for-Sugar was no more.

CHAPTER FIVE

# Alone in the Desert

I lay enclosed in a cocoon of red pain, surrounded by a pulsating
womb of agony. Every part of my body ached and throbbed
while my head seemed to swell with the everwidening ripples
that travelled outwards and outwards from the splashing stone of
my existence. Slowly I became conscious of each individual pain
and of the overwhelming fact that I was alive.

But was I alive? Frenchie was dead. Roy and Aussie were dead.
Perhaps I too was dead, and the pain just the beginning of my
punishment in purgatory. I lay still, with the throbbing rhythm of
pain in my head, overlaid by the tickling sensation of countless flies
that crawled all over my bleeding face. Slowly I drifted into a semi-
conscious state of daydreaming.

I'd entered the mess that morning, just one of an air-crew passing
through. There had been a strange card underneath my plate
marked with a blackened cross.

"It means you're a coffin-bearer, old son," I was told by one of the
old hands. "Hudson crashed last night as usual."

We'd met outside the sergeants' mess and were picked up by a
dusty jeep that took us to the morgue. Our first job was to load the
coffins, for bodies putrefied quickly in that heat.

*Would I have a coffin? I was in the desert now, and so would have no
coffin at all.*

Those coffins were not very elaborate things, merely made of the
remains of old packing cases. As I travelled to the cemetery, I
studied the long V-shaped cracks between the planks and wondered
whether you could see from inside there. A baked-bean tin had been
hammered flat and the name punched out with a centre punch.

So a Hudson had crashed while on anti-submarine patrol, and there I was travelling to the cemetery in a jeep, while at my feet was a completely unknown Sgt. Parker.

Here, in my delirium of pain, I remembered that journey through the African backwoods. There was luscious green growth, and soft moist sand, and little red and black birds, and phone wires attached to the necks of beer bottles bolted to tree-trunks.

The graves had been dug for the four airmen, and a firing squad stood at ease and smoking to one side. Beyond was a bugler whispering to the padre while the official photographer with his camera on spindly legs prepared to record the scene for the grieving relatives at home. They all sprang to attention as the jeep arrived. I had never carried a coffin before and was surprised to discover how heavy it was and how it cut into my shoulder. Carefully we made our way to the grave-side where we placed the coffins on baulks of timber laid across the mouth of the grave. Draped between the timbers were two strong ropes. I looked down at the one at my feet to figure out how the coffin would be lowered. The short service was completed, a sharp command brought the firing squad into position, a rattle of rifle fire echoed through the trees, the bugler played *The Last Post*, and the photographer hid himself underneath his black velvet cover.

The padre held the corner of the Union Jack and looked knowingly at the bearers and I, copying the others, bent down and picked up my rope's end. We all took the weight of the coffin, and the two timbers were removed. Hand over hand we gently lowered the sergeant into the ground.

It wasn't that I did anything very wrong. After all, I should've been warned not to step off the plank lining the grave. The coffin was heavy and I took a step forward to gain extra purchase on the rope, but unfortunately it was the rainy season, and the ground was sodden. Slowly the side of the grave caved in, depositing me on my hands and knees at the bottom with the coffin on its end beside me.

For a moment all was confusion while the other bearers tried to straighten out the casket, which was difficult with me by its side. The warrant officer in charge of the bearers leaned over and offered a helping hand, but he too underestimated the slippery nature of the ground and instead of pulling me out, I pulled the warrant officer in.

Everything now was in utter confusion. The side of the grave had broken away to an angle of 45 degrees and anyone standing on that treacherous ramp would end in the sticky quagmire at the bottom of the grave. Eventually someone threw in a rope and the firing squad pulled away like sailors hoisting the anchor, although this time it was the warrant officer and me.

… Once again, I became aware of my pain. Cautiously I moved just one of my legs and my arm. They seemed to work, but was it not true that amputated limbs lived on within the brain? Perhaps I had lost both arms and legs, and my movements were just fantasy? What would life be like without limbs? I groaned and the enveloping curtain came down to engulf me once again.

Slowly I became aware of a comforting smell. It was a mixture of disinfectant and damp books. I recognised it immediately as the smell of my school. I looked down and thought that I could see Peggy, Peggy Hall. There she sat beside me, as she had for a very long time. I could plainly see her with her hair brushed back into a bun, reading her book with her steel-rimmed glasses. Suddenly the vision changed and she was standing in front of me with her hair free and flowing in shiny waves over her shoulders as she looked at me with eyes that for the first time I could see were pools of deepest blue.

"Tell me the story of the ugly duckling, Billy." "Once upon a time there was a duck, or was it a swan, no, a duck. It had raised a clutch of baby chicks that were all the same except for one. This little duck was different and so was compelled to swim at the back of the long file as they followed their mother. She was so depressed that one day she swam away on her own. Soon she was in a shady pool where the water was still and quiet. She looked down at her reflection and to her surprise she found she was not a duck at all but a beautiful swan."

"Am I an ugly duckling, Billy-boy?" She laughed and disappeared.

I felt a little better the next time I forced my eyes open, only to quickly shut them as the blinding light of the sun seared through. Turning my head to one side, I opened them again. I seemed to be lying on the ground: I had crashed, and I was still alive.

As I fell into a disturbed sleep, my life for the moment was saved by a simple shadow, for as the sun moved round my inert body became shaded by the pinnacle of rock behind. Without this, my fever would have continued until I died. It was late afternoon when I next awoke, as the sun was drooping towards the horizon sending long shadows across the sand. I lay for a while and slowly took stock of my position. There did not seem to be any bones broken, even though every muscle ached with bruises. I sat up with my neck against the rock's face and looked about. All around were gigantic rocky outcrops towering high in the air, like a scene from some ancient time. Tinted pink and yellow by the oxides in the soil, everywhere they rose in a series of grotesque shapes from the desert floor.

I seemed to be about 20 feet up upon a ledge, and from where I sat the featureless sand stretched from the horizon to the foot of the outcrops like the sea slowly drowning a Hebridean island. The plane seemed to have struck and disintegrated at the top of a solitary stack of rock 100 yards ahead. I figured that I must have been thrown in a gigantic parabola, landing on the ledge instead of falling to the sand below. I remembered the two gunners – they had been alive; but as I stared around, steadying myself with the rock, it was obvious that no one else could have survived that crash. The sand all around was littered with the debris from the wrecked aircraft, and had I fallen to the sand I would no doubt have been killed. Yet not only was my fall arrested by the rock, but by some strange trick of luck I had been cushioned by my parachute.

As I gazed around at the layered rock that looked like petrified teeth in a giant's jaw, and then beyond at the circular horizon, the real truth of my situation became clear. I'd had a lucky escape, of that there was no doubt, but was it an escape or just a delay of the inevitable? No food, no water, and no one knowing of my position, what chance had I of survival? I stood and peered down the rock face. Even if I succeeded in getting down, there seemed little point in the effort: I might just as well sit there quietly and await the end.

There was, however, something stirring within me that made me reject such a negative attitude. Perhaps I was doomed, but I was determined to fight to the last. By now the sun had become big and red and the sky began to glow in every tone from orange through to crimson. If I was going to move, I must do so quickly or be marooned on the ledge for the night. However, there was a great difference between planning to get down and achieving it: even 20 feet is a long way when one has no experience as a rock-climber. The decision was taken out of my hands by the sudden onset of darkness. One moment the sun seemed to be floating like a balloon on the horizon, and the next it had disappeared.

My bruised body sapped my strength and as I lay wondering if I had any future at all, I drifted into a half-asleep, half-awake condition where the night slowly wore on. I was surprised by the beauty of the stars. Never before had the sky looked like an enormous dome, but now it curved all around to the horizon, clear and easy to see. At home I had an encyclopaedia where the constellations were drawn like people and animals, and now for once I could see some sense in it all.

What really surprised me was the intense cold. As I lay huddled in my sheepskin flying jacket, idly identifying the Pole Star, low on the horizon compared with it at home, I shivered and rubbed my hands.

What I needed was an extra blanket. My mother was always asking about it at night. There on the table would be my night-time cup of cocoa, the powder, sugar, and milk, mixed to a smooth paste in the bottom of the cup, and I knew that no sooner had I heated the water than Mum would call down the stairs.

"If you need another blanket, there is one in the cupboard."

It was that thought that brought to my attention the pack of my parachute. It had been reasonably soft as a pillow, but of course it was packed with white silk, yards and yards of it. That, I remembered, was a good insulator and would help to keep me warm.

It was very dark, but as I was used to roaming in the country in the dark winter evenings, this held no worries for me. Carefully holding the top of the pack with one hand, I pulled the rip cord with the other. The pack jumped beneath my hands as the pent-up silk expanded to its natural size. I opened the four flaps flat on the rock and pulled the silk towards me. Soon I was fast asleep.

The sun rose, changing – in the space of an hour the bitter cold of the night into a warm dawn, to be followed by the usual searing heat of the day. The rocky stack was directly in line with the sun which, as it rose, cast a shadow like that of a gigantic sun-dial shortening and rotating until the ledge of rock where I was sleeping gradually moved into full sunshine.

I instinctively curled down inside the mass of white parachute silk to escape the rays of the sun. I lay there for some time planning my next move. I consciously noticed the tremendous difference the reflecting power of the silk gave to my comfort, and resolved to take it with me when I left. But of course I knew that my first problem was to climb down from the ledge. Forcing myself to brave the sun, I screwed up my eyes to protect them from the glare. The ledge had not completely lost its shadow, so I quickly sought protection. I noticed the open canvas satchel of my parachute. It had lain throughout the night in a small saucer-shaped depression in the rock, and the heavy dew had condensed on the canvas. I could hardly believe my eyes. I had expected mirages, but this was too detailed and too close for that. Perhaps my mind was playing tricks, for it seemed too incredible to be true. Bending down, I sipped; then, with a slobbering noise like a wine-taster testing a wine, I drank it before the sun returned it back to the air from which it had come.

The water seemed to restore my senses, for I stood up against the rock and looked around. Apart from scattered debris, there was little sign of the plane; but I did notice that littering the desert was the charred remains of a major tank battle. I stared at a tank that was gutted from a major explosion. Further away were others, even a huge lorry that seemed minus its back wheel, all rapidly becoming buried in the featureless sand.

But how to get down was the first problem, and then I noticed the ropes from my chute. If I could tie them together, I was sure they would stretch to the floor. They were made of nylon, and thin, but would easily take my weight. I sat down and started undoing all the hitches. Soon I had made a rope with knots every foot. The next problem was to find something to use as an anchorage. Above me, I noticed a stone jammed into a crack in the rock, and it was the work of a minute to attach my rope to that and then throw the rest over the edge.

I was surprised to discover when I reached the desert floor that it was not as flat as it had appeared to be. Dunes, 20 or 30 feet high, stretched everywhere; and for the first time I realised that I had no idea of which way I needed to go.

I remembered the escape compass I had on my trousers, two little buttons on my flies. Using a piece of sharp rock, I hacked away at the thread until they came off in my hands. One had a small speck of white on its face. I carefully placed one button upside down on a rock and then the other the right way up, where a small bump in the centre of the upside-down button fitted exactly into a small recess on the other, forming an almost frictionless pivot. I carefully spun the button and watched as it slowly came to a stop with the white spot showing north.

A burning on the back of my neck reminded me of the need for the parachute, and quickly I wrapped myself from top to bottom in the shining white silk. Over my head, my neck, and my body went fold after fold of the lightweight material, until my face was the only area unprotected.

I looked to the east and discovered that a route in that direction would lead right across the first dune. Just my luck, I thought; however, I should get a better view from the top. But that dune turned out to be only one of many, and as I dragged myself up them one by one, the torture became so intense as to be almost unbearable.

Soon I came to understand exactly what a desert dune was. I discovered that the downwind side of each one was made of sand hard-packed for centuries. In many cases this was quite sheer and I had to pick myself up on all fours, which meant tying my robes in large knots around my waist. Once I reached the top, the surface would become suddenly soft and I would find myself up to my knees in the loose sand. It was so loose, in fact, that it seemed to act like soft snow.

On this loose surface, I found that it took all my effort to move at all. I noticed that whenever I lifted a leg the footprint immediately filled with sand pouring in like miniature avalanches, so that my steps quickly disappeared without trace. I turned to find that no mark indicated my occupation of that unscrutable landscape.

That fact more than anything else showed the desperate nature of my plight. Forcing it to the back of my mind, I tried to walk on. I found that every step meant a continuing dragging weight upon my feet, and every step involved a time-consuming effort to lift my feet high enough to avoid the clinging sand. Soon I dreaded each step I took, for it always seemed to end in the agony of sliding downhill, my flying boots filling with scalding grains. As I staggered forward it seemed that life was just rock and sand, and sand and rock.

Thoughts poured through my mind in an endless stream until gradually, in spite of all my conscious efforts, I began to feel depressed. As the sun rose higher and the dunes became steeper, I began to drown in my current of unsuppressible thoughts, and I began to realise that all this was just an utter waste of time. I sat down on a rock and automatically emptied the sand first from one boot and then the other, and then standing up I took off my parachute and deliberately folded it properly and draped it around myself in a more comfortable way. I thought about the Bedouin and how they swathed their bodies from the burning sun; then, pretending to be someone from *The Desert Song*, I surveyed the land around. My direct line eastwards, I noticed, was up an enormous dune – quite the biggest I had seen. Did I have the strength to clamber to the top? Surely I might just as well turn to the left and walk along the clean, wind-swept slabs between the dunes? After all, perhaps soon there would be shade as the giant blocked the sun. I stood up and staggered off to the left but could not help feeling that this was failure: I was not walking a straight line; I was wandering aimlessly about the desert.

I looked up at the overhanging escarpment and noted that it was steeper than any I had climbed before. And then I had an idea: perhaps I could somehow reach the top, then I might see something that had until now been below the horizon.

"I'll do it," I shouted defiantly, and a little cascade of sand grains began to pour over my boot. "Do you hear?" I shouted, "I'm going to do it."

The climb was a nightmare of effort and endurance, but every time I felt like giving up I remembered that over the top would be salvation. And then – I made it! I staggered to the top and looked around. But there was nothing, nothing but dune succeeding dune in the diminishing sizes of perspective.

"Oh God, I'm lost," I cried, and sank to my knees sobbing.

"Help me, Mummy, help me," I cried, but this time there was no parent to help; now I was on my own. And yet was I on my own? I buried my face in my arms and as I knelt there fighting off waves of unconsciousness I could see in my mind's eye myself kneeling but this time by my bed with my mother at my side.

"God bless Mummy and Daddy, and Granny and Granddad, and make me a good boy, for Jesus Christ's sake, Amen. Oh God," I said, "Help me, please help me, save me, for Jesus Christ's sake, Amen". It seemed right to end the prayer like that, and so I repeated the litany over and over again. I could feel beneath my arms the hard angle iron beneath the frame of my bed at home.

## CHAPTER SIX

# Rescue

The sky began to change colour and the wind blew hot and sticky, like a breath from the open oven of the bakers at home, but I was drifting in a sea of memory. I remembered being on holiday once, when I had become lost. I had wandered around in the rain; this time, it was not rain but sand. Clouds of dust enveloped me, making me cough and splutter. Instinctively I turned my back to the wind, with little effect. I kept my mouth tightly closed and yet my teeth still became gritty. Covering my face with the silk of the parachute, I attempted to filter the air, and for the first time I realised I was sweating, sweating all over. Then, when my face was covered with mud from the sand and sweat, the dust fog blew away, stopping as quickly as it had begun. The sky had changed from a blue to a red muddy colour and I could see the sun as a gleaming disc surrounded by a border of blue.

I stood on the crest of a dune and shook the loose sand from my robes. For a time the sun's glare was reduced and my visibility improved, and it was then that I noticed the small dune ahead. Was it my imagination, or was there a deep shadow at its base? Yes, I was sure of it: a small crevice where I could stay until the sun had lost its heat. Anywhere would do to escape the blazing sun. Even then I was not sure, and in my excitement I lost my balance and rolled down the dune in a flurry of sand.

The wind had played strange tricks at times, but my eyes were not deceiving me and this dune was definitely undercut. I bent down and could see that the crack went deep into the dune, getting smaller and smaller as it went. Without thinking of the risk of getting stuck, I lay on the hot sand and edged myself into the fissure.

It was not until I was in the shade and my head barely a few inches from the roof that I realised what I had done. I closed my eyes and felt sick at the thought of all those thousands of tons of sand that could collapse and suffocate me.

A strange metallic smell set my mind wandering. I remembered the blacksmith's forge.

The blacksmith was working and I enjoyed peering in. The entrance to the lane was a stable door and the smith kept the bottom half-bolted, so I leaned over, resting my arms along the top, enjoying the familiar smells of rust and smoke and horse manure. It was so dark and gloomy in there after the sun outside. Half-visible racks held lengths of rusty iron of every dimension, while near the door was a pile of pick-axe heads and bits and pieces of farm machinery. On the wall opposite hung medieval instruments of torture. In the centre was the only thing that had a metallic sheen: the anvil. Right at the back, elevated on a 3-foot high platform, was the fire. It appeared to be made of little black peas with a red heart in the centre. As I watched the smith pumped the bellows, and the fire exploded into a cascade of red, then white, while a volcano of sparks shot into the air.

I watched as the smith removed from the fire a piece of red-hot iron. He placed it on the anvil, gave it a few taps and plunged it into a tank of water where it hissed, sending up a cloud of steam that added to the underworld effect. He looked up and noticed me,

"You here again? You can't seem to stay away. Tell you what – how would you like to work with me on Saturdays?"

"Yes please."

"Right then, I'll pay you … let me see, how about two shillings for a full day?"

"Yes, thank you." Two whole shillings! Why, that was nearly a week's wages on the papers.

"Now it's important that you come along very early this Saturday, because I have a big job on and need all the help I can get."

Then I had a sudden thought. "I've got to do my paper round first."

"O.K. As soon as you finish will do. You'll have to pump the bellows."

I grinned to myself. Pumping bellows, I was used to that.

Bill in his schooldays at his primary school in Thatcham, Berks (he is the pupil nearest bottom right).

Naval cadet Bill shows his little brother Philip and his Dad James, around the training ship *Warspite* which was moored on the Thames until it was decommissioned in 1940.

Bill in naval uniform, before his RAF career, seen at home on leave in his mother's garden.

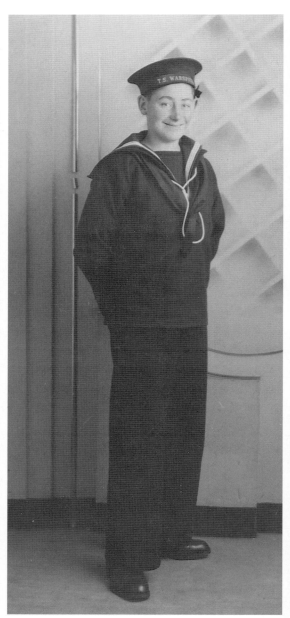

Bill as a boy cadet on the training ship *Warspite*.

Bill with his Aunt Georgina at the family home.

An early shot of a proud
young Bill in uniform.

Learning to fly during pilot
training.

With fellow RAF sergeants relaxing before duty on an airfield (Bill is the one without his cap).

Bombing-up a Wellington.
(*RAF 214 FMS Squadron*)

A typical briefing from 1943.

A rare shot of a Wellington radio.
(*RAF 214 FMS Squadron*)

Photo taken by Bill of a casualty of war. Bill was a keen photographer even in wartime.

On leave with his mother, Florence.

Bill pictured with his wings and stripes outside the family home in Thatcham.

Bill's wife Gwen in her younger years. Before the war she worked in the Civil service.

Gwen in WAAF uniform.

Gwen was a Met assistant in the war. Here she is seen plotting a chart for the Met Officer to produce his forecast.

1 June 1946. Bill and Gwen marry at St Mary's Parish Church in Broadwater, Worthing.

An early portrait of Bill in RAF uniform.

So I completed my walk home, singing as I went.

Two shillings – that would make a big difference to Mother. The smith did not know that I had more experience at pumping than any boy in the village. For a long time, for two pence a service I had pumped the organ in the church. I had to squeeze into a narrow gallery at the back that had a wooden bench along the wall. Extending out from the wall was a handle that had to be moved up and down to fill the bellows. From the ceiling hung a string that ended in a little bobbin. When the bellows were full, the bobbin hung level with a mark on the wall; when empty, it hung opposite a higher mark.

After a while I knew just how much air the organist would need for a verse and so did not worry too much about the marks, and that was my downfall. On the last occasion I had come across an old prayer book and discovered at the back a table that could be used to find the date of Easter. I was so busy that I failed to notice that the organist had decided to end with a triumphant fanfare. With four finger chords on both hands and almost all the stops out, the drain on the air supply was enormous. I, however, had my head in the book and did not notice the ominous movement of the bobbin. In the middle of a glorious burst of sound, the organ faded away with the sound of a lovesick cow. I was not allowed to pump the organ again.

My first day with the smith was spent pumping the fire, holding the horses, and fetching and carrying. I was in heaven. "You've done well, boy. You've used your initiative and I'm pleased. Here's your two bob. I think I will be able to turn you into a blacksmith yet."

This memory was now so poignant that I could remember the strong smell of rusty iron. It was overpoweringly strong. I opened my eyes and studied the ceiling above. I scratched away at the sand. I tapped it and it rang like iron as well as smelling like it, and so I scratched more and more until there was no doubt about it: it was the under body of a car.

I lay there for a while only vaguely interested in my discovery, for it was all becoming so pointless. All the agony of my journey and my complete exhaustion were an utter waste of time. If I had stayed on my rocky ledge I would no doubt by now be dead, but what had I gained for all my efforts? Another 24 hours of life? But could *this* be called life? My tongue was swollen between cracked and ulcerated lips; my face and legs were burning from the scalding sand; all for what reason? It was only postponing the inevitable. Huddled in the shadow, I closed my eyes in complete despair.

I was woken by the sun shining into my refuge. It was now low on the horizon and sending long shadows across the desert. I looked up at the shell of the car and my curiosity stirred. Was it just possible that there was food, and water in there? It took a painful effort to roll out into the full light of the day. I could see that the dune was a covering of sand over the car, smoothing out its harsh outline into a flat featureless heap, so bending down I started scraping the sand away.

It was not a car but an old van. Obviously, with one side bogged down in loose sand, it had been left to rot by the retreating army. Clearing the sand away from the back, I found it an easy matter to open the door, for in that climate things took a long time to rust. A whiff of stale air and acid greeted me as I clambered inside and looked around.

It took a while for my eyes to adjust to the gloom, but I could just make out that the side of the van seemed to have a small bench with dials and meters set in the surface, while the wall above was covered with tools all clipped in their places. On the floor was red and black wire that had become unravelled from the reels on the bench. The other side, near me, seemed to be covered with a pile of black metallic boxes. I knew what they were all right. I had found a deserted radio repair shop, and immediately the idea flashed through my mind that I could radio for help.

However, I thought, my first job must be food.

Would there be any food in a workshop like this? I could dimly make out the outline of a small hatch that seemed to lead to the driver's position, so I clambered over the wire and pushed my way through. It was the driver's compartment, but I found that I had to clamber over a bunk bed to reach the steering wheel, and it was there that I found what I was looking for: a carton of tins that I recognised as sardines.

I opened two before I was sick, the olive oil after my period of starvation being too much to digest. It did, however, give me a period when I could take stock of the situation. As I looked at the tins that were left, I noticed that they were alongside a great deal of empty packaging, and it dawned upon me that the soldiers had raided the rations before leaving. I realised that my life may have been spared by the soldier's dislike of sardines.

My good fortune with food caused me to look around for water. I turned and went back into the workshop and nearly stumbled over a jerrycan of acid. I picked it up, placed it to one side, and then looked at it again. An idea flashed through my mind. Batteries, acid – surely that should mean distilled water? A plastic container shed its load of fine sand as I dragged it from underneath the bench. I could tell it was liquid, but it was too dangerous to drink any old liquid in a workshop. I forced myself to drag it to the door where I could study the label carefully. I knew no German but was confident I understood "Wasser destillieries".

"There is no doubt," I thought, "but the last few days in the van have made a difference." I couldn't really remember how long for all the time had been a nightmare. I looked out of the side window that now peered along a tunnel of sand, and noted that once again it was being blocked from the outside.

With the sand all around insulating the cab from the heat, and light provided through the holes that I had scraped, life seemed quite tolerable. The cracks on my hands were healing, my blistered feet were now giving me no pain, and I had acclimatised myself to the heat. Gradually I found that it was best to work in the few hours at sunset and sunrise, for then, just for a while, it was actually pleasant outside.

In fact it was not only my body that had been restored, but my mind, for I had come to terms with the situation. I could think of all the events since the crash in a detached way, as if they had happened to someone else, as though I were merely an observer. I knew that by all standards I should have been dead by now. I alone had survived the crash, I alone had staggered off into the desert in the searing heat of the day, and I alone had survived. As for the future, well, that was limited; but somehow my mind would not concentrate on the future, for I was a man with two time dimensions only: the past and – more importantly – the present.

After my ravishing of the first two tins of sardines, I rationed myself to only half a tin a day, but I knew very well that even then my time was strictly limited. Of one thing I was certain: I was not going to stagger off into the sun at its hottest time again. No, the sensible thing seemed to me to stay on the bunk and slowly sleep my time away. I had heard stories of submariners doing that, and with limited food I was in a similar position. In fact, I discovered that after suffering pangs of hunger on the first day, I gradually developed the power to cut my intake down to less and less as the days went by.

And yet all the time there was the feeling at the back of my mind that perhaps I was not doing enough. I sat up and leaned against the bulkhead, scratching my beard that by now was beginning to itch.

"Suppose," I said to myself, for I had got into the habit of talking aloud, "suppose we argue that it's curtains for me. Then I seem to have two choices: one is to stay here and die in comfort, and the other is to start walking and die in pain."

"Now, let's work out the chances of survival. If I stay here, the odds are nil; but if I walk, who knows?" And that was the point that nagged me. I had heard of people dying when there was help just around the corner. Did I know what was over the next dune? I seemed to remember a story about Scott of the Antarctic, where when the blizzard cleared his little red tent turned out to have been only a few yards from the base camp.

I had discovered that I could tell the time of day by the length of shadow at the window, and I now looked up and decided that the sun was low enough for me to venture outside. I climbed up the dune to the top of the van and looked around. The usual sandy hillocks were still there. I noticed that the sand was blowing off the van roof, laying bare the roof-rack and the circular ring of the direction-finding aerial. I decided to heap the sand back, for already I had noticed its life-saving insulating properties. With a last look at the red disc of the sun, I slid down the dune and burrowed my way in through the back door of the van. I had learned to live by the sun, and knew that I had a little while before the twilight disappeared with dramatic suddenness.

Starting at one end of the van, I methodically opened every cupboard and drawer in idle curiosity. My technical knowledge of radio was almost nonexistent, but as I fiddled with wire and meters

I was convinced that if I only knew there must be a way to contact the outside world. Perhaps if I knew German it would help, but although I could recognise the meaning of some of the labels, I could not understand the books that I found in a cupboard. I took one of the books back to my bunk, and in the fading light leafed through the pages. Not only was it in a foreign language, but it was printed in a ridiculous way. The type was very black and old-fashioned, and to me it looked almost like that used by Caxton.

It was the next day that I came upon something I recognised. Strapped to the wall, high up and behind a pile of old junk, was an old photographer's tripod and a set of semaphore flags. I took them down and studied them with interest.

The semaphore flags reminded me of an incident when I was a seaman in a ship in convoy.

I was at the wheel when the Captain came out of the chart-room.

"Bailey, do you know how to send semaphore?"

"Yes, sir."

"Good – then I'll get the relief man to take over the wheel and then you can send a message to the escort. As you know, we have not been equipped with an Aldis lamp, and with strict radio silence it is the only way we have of sending a message."

I handed over the wheel and entered the chartroom, where the captain was busy extracting some dusty semaphore flags from the back of a cupboard.

"Take these and stand on the monkey island and attract their attention."

Soon a flash answered the waving flags.

"Send, crew member very ill." As I sent the message letter by letter, an answering flash came at the end of every word.

"Stomach pains, pulse rate fast, respiration slow, diarrhoea."

"How do you spell *diarrhoea*?"

"Send 'shits' boy, 'with much blood'."

I came down much relieved at my successful mission, as it was the first time since leaving the training ship that I had used my skill. As I was winding up the flags, the wireless officer came dashing up the stairs.

"We're expecting a message, Sparks, so will you check what they send?"

The escort began flashing rapidly, and soon the captain and chief officer were out of their depths. At the end the three went into the chart room where they had a discussion. After a while the captain came out and called "Bailey."

I joined them and they all looked at me.

"Bailey, the sixth engineer is dangerously ill. He ought to be sent to hospital, but that is quite impossible. The only thing we can do is to give him morphia to relieve his pain. I want you to start a 24-hour watch over him, so go down to his cabin and let me know the moment there is any change."

The sixth engineer's cabin was aft, deep down in the bowels of the ship and very close to the rotating shaft. When I entered, I discovered it to be a dark coffin of a room with a bunk attached to one wall. On the opposite wall was an upholstered bench, and at the end was a set of three drawers. The only light was from a naked bulb that swung back and forth with the rolling of the ship. Everything in the room vibrated at the beat of the engines and the thud of the screws. Now and again, a sudden bang and another vibrating machine joined in as the steering engines turned the rudder here or there.

The sixth engineer turned restlessly and sometimes cried out in an animal-like way.

I took a magazine from a pile on top of the drawers. It was an out of date *Practical Mechanics*, obviously collected by the poor man in the bunk.

It was in the third spell, around three in the morning, when I was aware of a change in the chap on the bed. He seemed strangely still. I stood up and reluctantly studied the man. I had never seen a dead man before, but I was sure he had died. Quickly I dashed up the stairs into the dark of the blacked-out ship. Suddenly a white presence wrapped itself around my face. In panic I tugged at the clammy material, only to find it was a cloth hung out to dry by the cook. With my heart in my mouth I ran to the bridge.

"I think he's died, sir," I said to the officer of the watch.

Later the bosun and his mate entered the cabin with a roll of new canvas. They spread the canvas out and placed the body in the centre, then after placing a broken rusty wheel upon his chest they began sewing up the body. By tradition, the bosun sewed over his face while the mate sewed from the feet. By tradition also, they were given a bottle of rum as a reward for their efforts.

Next morning I helped to unship the mess table from its legs. It was then taken onto the after tank tops and stood upon two wooden boxes, pointing outboard.

All hands were called on deck and stood around the table. The captain looked up at the bridge and the vibrating of the engines ceased. Soon everything was quiet except for the lapping of the sea against the still ship's side. The bosun and his mate moved forward and the canvas slid into the water with a splash. For a moment all was still and then the faint ring of the engineroom telegraph could be heard, the familiar vibration began to fill our world again and my friends and I took the table back to the mess room.

Here in the desert, it seemed that I had little use for the semaphore flags. But the photographer's tripod? It looked so old and grubby that it had probably never been moved since it was first made. But why in a radio workshop should there be an old Victorian tripod? All it needed was a huge box camera, a black velvet cloth and then, with a "Watch the birdie", a picture could be made. Perhaps if I rummaged around I could find the camera.

I continued the survey of my possessions, opening every container in the van until I came across another curiosity. It was a shaving mirror mounted on a brass stand and containing a little model of a telescope upon the top. I studied it with a smile on my face. Funny people, these Germans: it was obviously a trophy of some kind, but why a shaving mirror? Later in the day, though, I came across the tripod in a German manual. Yet it was not the text that held my attention but the apparatus on the top, for it looked very much like the presentation shaving mirror. Carefully I studied the caption, but it meant little to me. The Gothic script made the words difficult to understand, and yet there was something familiar about one of the words: SPIEGELTELEGRAPHIE. It was the "telegraph" bit that seemed to ring a bell. I stared at the picture, for there was something about it that reminded me of the past.

And then it came back! In a flash, I remembered a picture in an old book long ago. I remembered the picture clearly now: it was of two soldiers in the 1914 war. There they were, dressed in their puttees and staring intently forward as they operated such a device.

Yes there was no doubt; it was a heliograph, a device for sending messages by the sun. With trembling hands I went about fixing the mirror to the tripod. With the illustration to help me, I found it quite easy. The telescope was to focus on a distant station, and the lever at the side deflected the mirror a few degrees to make a flash of sunshine. What a stroke of luck that I could remember my Morse! I could hardly wait for the heat to go out of the sun before I was on the roof, eager to flash out my S.O.S.

But although it seemed a good idea, the featureless landscape of dunes and sand made it impossible to direct my signal in any particular direction. Soon I was flashing a message, then moving it slightly, then again, until I had completed a circle of the horizon. It was a thankless task, and soon I had degraded my message into a meaningless series of flashes.

It was comforting, though, to have a routine, and so I would signal for a period in the early morning, then another in the late afternoon, and then spend the rest of the day dozing on the bunk. It was while I was laying down, idly leafing through yet another manual, that I suddenly had a terrible thought. Suppose while I was inside a relief party passed by. They would not know I was there. What I had to do was to display a signal of some sort. After a few minutes, I remembered an aluminium telescopic aerial. I could hoist that with a flag.

I picked up the mast from under the bench and studied it carefully. It should do the trick ... but what about a flag? Of course, the old and trusted parachute would do well. Taking a knife from its clip on the wall, I cut a large square from the bottom, including the eyelets normally used for the harness. Using lengths of flex I tied the silk to the aerial, and then carrying my snips and a reel of wire I mounted the roof of the van. The circular direction-finding aerial seemed the ideal position, so I quickly lashed it upright across the diameter and soon it was waving gaily in the breeze.

It was the next day when I suddenly heard a voice. "If there's anyone in there, come out now."

I quickly scrambled to my feet and crawled out of the door to stand blinking in the bright sun.

"Hands above your head. Now turn round."

I turned to see that behind me was a soldier with a rifle pointed at my stomach.

"Who are you?" "Sergeant Bailey. R.A.F."

The soldier relaxed and, lowering his rifle, said:

"Its O.K. lads, he's one of ours."

I watched, astounded, as soldiers appeared from behind boulders and dunes. They gathered round as I felt the world spin. My knees crumbled and I sank to the ground.

Corporal Finch, platoon commander of the Long Range Desert Patrol, looked at me.

"Let's go, the sooner we get him to an M.O. the better."

## CHAPTER SEVEN

# The Flight Commander's Story

It was hot, hellishly hot, and Flight-Lieutenant Gerald de Courcy could feel a trickle of perspiration running down his face. As it gathered momentum he dammed it with a quick wipe of his handkerchief, while he could feel his shirt wet and cold between his shoulder blades. He knew that the wet patches beneath his arms were growing. He was sweating and smelling like a pig; without doubt they were in for a sandstorm. It was funny how the humidity changed just before a storm: the air seemed to give up its job of evaporating moisture, as if to say that the carriage of countless grains of sand was quite enough for one day.

He looked at the sergeant in front of him and wriggled in his chair.

"I don't know about you," he went on, "but it seems abominably hot – I just can't stop sweating. This is my second shirt today. My batman will moan, for you know what flies do to all the laundry around here. It probably means that a sandstorm is on its way. Did you sweat at all when you were in the desert?"

"I was only conscious of it once, sir – and you're right, as that was just before a storm."

"Yes, it's the humidity you know … but to get back to business, I can't say how pleased I am to see you back. You were posted as missing".

He studied the lad intently, taking in his red and swollen face with the cracked and broken lips. He noticed the bleached and lifeless hair, and the tell-tale indicators of strain in the twitching eyes. But when he had said he cared, it was not just an idle statement; for out of all the squadron he seemed to be the only chap that felt these things. Others might operate efficiently, on the level of aircraft availability and duty rotas; but when the aircraft returned (or failed to return), and the profit-and-loss account balanced, he was always worried about the wasteful squander of human life. He always wrote to the next of kin. It was not necessary of course, but somehow he felt it was something he wanted to do. He knew how he would feel when that telegram arrived. Surely the folks at home were entitled to some explanation. A line from a poem that appealed to him sprang into his mind.

"So was one life spent of many,
In a mouthful of sand in the desert."

If a letter from him would help, then he just must write, for the lives were real, and demanded more than a short telegram.

Perhaps that was why he always felt apart from air-crew members of his flight. It seemed as though they had no thoughts at all beyond everyday living; indeed, perhaps that was not a bad philosophy for the nature of their existence. But he was always searching for meaning beyond just living, he wanted to know just why we were here.

Like the sergeant, for example: what had made this young country lad leave his home and his friends to attempt to annihilate people he had never met, and to risk oblivion as equally remote strangers tried to kill him? He had asked one or two at the beginning, but they always gave the same banal answers, so that he had given up enquiring by now. He knew why he was here: it was because his life was crumbling, eroded by the evil black cloud sweeping across Europe.

For to him, the war was a crusade, for he had personally seen the blank faces of the Jews, and had been present at the devastation of Warsaw, and he knew beyond doubt that his life was finished; that the map of his Europe had been rolled up and locked away for ever. But then, perhaps he had been luckier than most; for, as a pianist, his life had been spent in practice and travel. For a time he had practised harder than ever in an attempt to block out reality, but it was of no use; Bach and Chopin seemed swept away by the maelstrom of events.

Of course he never played piano now. The last time had been in Kabrit on the beer-stained upright. He had opened the lid and, as his hands fingered the familiar chords, his mind went back to his very first concert in Cheltenham. He'd been quite surprised to find that men had quietly left the barside to gather on the floor around him, some with tears in their eyes.

He glanced at the dog-eared photo on his table:

Moira, his wife, had understood.

"If you feel you should go, then you have my blessing," she had said. He remembered the last time they had visited Heidelberg. There had seemed, even then, a stench of corruption over the city. Of course the view over the Neckar was as charming as ever, and the coffee on the veranda overlooking the river had been the same; but was it just imagination, or was the waiter insolent? Perhaps the waiter knew that not a dozen miles from them, the Krupps factories were working overtime?

The concert the previous evening had started well, in fact he had never played better; and yet he could sense that the audience was never with him. He could feel the restlessness, and perhaps that was why he had finished with a Chopin polonaise. They had listened in silence, and he left the stage defiant and alone. It was then that it had dawned upon him that something must be done. He was sure that the canker must be cut away, cut away by personal sacrifice, sacrifice of his career, and if necessary his life. And yet – was he prepared to make that final offer? He looked at the sergeant in front of him. He had been tried, but Gerald's turn was yet to come.

"When you were walking through the desert, did you feel afraid?"

"Part of the time, sir, but mostly I felt – well, uncomfortable. It's difficult to describe, it was … painful."

He nodded; he thought he understood, for the one way of pushing fear to one side was to concentrate hard on other things. It was an almost universal thought around here. But did he really understand? He realised that, young though the sergeant was, he now stood apart: he had experienced something extraordinary and would never be the same again. How had Eliot put it,

"He had seen the eternal footman hold his coat and snicker."

There was no doubt the lad had changed, and as he stood there Gerald could sense stillness, a calmness that he had not noticed before.

"Yes, I know what you mean," he said aloud.

"How long do you think you could have survived in that van?"

"When I was rescued, I had 2 days left." "Did that not scare you?"

"I'd grown to live with it, sir. All my comrades were gone, so why should I be different? I decided that the next day I would start writing my experiences. At school I was very interested in the story of Scott in the Antarctic. He did that, and I felt that perhaps someone would find the story later."

"But while you were in the van, didn't you realise that you'd soon starve?"

"Yes, but somehow it didn't seem to matter."

"How long have you been in the R.A.F., Sergeant?"

"Less than a year sir, I did my L.T.W. at Babbacombe, E.F.T.S. at Halton, and my S.F.T.S. at Little Rissington. After that I did my O.T.U. at Harwell."

"So you were completely U.K. trained, isn't that unusual?"

"Yes sir, I think we were the last intake to complete in England."

"Was that an advantage, do you think?"

"It was certainly more difficult, for during training we had to cope with fog and barrage balloons, while navigation in England was far harder than that in South Africa or Canada." Gerald smiled as he remembered his own efforts at map-reading over the Home Counties.

"Another thing – it was shorter, sir, we just went from one course to another."

Gerald studied him intently. "You surprise me. You've certainly packed a lot into your last year. Now I understand that you'll be in sick-bay for a while. When the M.O. thinks you're well enough he will give you a medical board, and then when you've passed that report back to me, and we'll set about finding you a new crew. I think you have shown considerable resource, but there is no doubt that you were very, very lucky."

He watched as the young man dipped under the flap and disappeared into the sunshine. He wondered what effect all this would have upon him. A pencil rolled off the table and he returned to reality to find that one leg of his table had slipped off its block and had sunk deep into the soft sand. He rammed it hard with his foot and picked up the book that went everywhere with him. He opened it at the dog-eared marker.

"This is a damned unnatural sort of war," he read, "The pilot sits among the clouds, quite sure / About the values he is fighting for."

He closed the book. He wasn't sure the poet was exactly right, for he wondered very much if the young sergeant was fighting for any values at all.

## CHAPTER EIGHT

# My New Crew

I was glad to get back on to flying duties. I enjoyed flying, and wandering around while grounded was boring. An edited edition of my adventure had swept the squadron, and all the pilots began to call me "Lucky Bill Bailey". Often they would ask me if my adventures had had any effect upon me. I always answered no, but in reality there was a difference – due not to the desert, but to them. When I came into the mess I would see them look at me and then talk among themselves. In a way I was a celebrity, and this built up my self-confidence; I felt I could cope with anything.

I was quite amused when I reported to the Flight Office to find that being called "Lucky Bill Bailey" had quite a useful effect. All the new air-crew were keen to fly with me; after all, who wouldn't want a skipper who was always lucky? Napoleon always asked of his new generals, "Is he lucky?"

This meant that I had the pick of them, and soon I was working up an excellent crew. They came together for the first time in their crew tent, where they all looked at me apprehensively.

"Well, chaps, here we are together for the first time, and I know you all feel scared. That's O.K., we all go through that – but you are my crew, and I am determined that we all become the best crew on the squadron. There's just one thing I would like to say and that's about my nick-name. It's all codswallop because you make your own luck in this game. You will soon find that all the other crews have strange rituals before flying, like bowing to the ground at all four points of the compass or pissing over the wheels, but I don't want any of that because the way to get through this is not by magic but by skill and concentration. I want all of us to really be good at our jobs and then think of others and be good as a crew. Now that's enough about me – let's find out all about each other."

I was secretly surprised at myself, for a few weeks ago I would not have spoken like that. Yet they all somehow expected it, wanting a dominant male to look after them. Most of them were about my age, except Wally the navigator. He came from Oxford, where he had completed his degree, but was quite happy to be told what to do. Chalky White the wireless operator was a scouser and would probably become the life and soul of the party. The two air gunners were small and came from Sheffield and Leeds, while the second pilot, John, was a strange choice, for he was rather timid and shy; but somehow he appealed to me, perhaps because we had some things in common.

When we started flying together, they all found that their skipper had some strange ideas. I always closed and clamped the entrance hatch myself, even though it was the second pilot's job, and I drilled poor John unmercifully over his technique with a photoflash. Practice, practice, practice until he could do the job blindfold, and even then he had to work against the clock until he could do it blindfold in one and a half minutes. It all seemed a bit ridiculous, but soon John began to be proud of his skill. It did mean that there was no hanging around over the target. We could make a bombing run, immediately do a 180-degree turn and drop a flash, and get out in a matter of minutes. As for my flying skill, they soon began to respect that; for the moment we were caught in searchlights, my manoeuvres were so extreme that they were petrified – in spite of the fact that I always managed to escape. They thought I also had another strange characteristic. After bombing, I refused to allow them to chat over the intercom, insisting that they concentrated all the way home. Most of our operations were against the harbour installations of Bizerta and Sousse, and it was not long before we were working like a well-oiled machine.

## CHAPTER NINE

# We are Attacked

I felt proud at the way my crew had settled down. For them, it had been in no way like my own baptism of fire over Tobruk, but nevertheless it could have been really dangerous. I was happy at the way they could reduce their exposure to fire to a minimum by the slick way they could take a picture. As I sat at the controls, I was amused at the silence on the intercom. It showed that they had taken my words to heart and were concentrating on lookout.

John was standing at the astrodome looking out for trouble overhead. Any minute now, I thought, I would hand over to him and have a little rest.

Then the silence was shattered by the excited voice of Titch the rear-gunner.

"Skipper, we're being followed." "Damn," I said. "Is it within range?"

"No, I don't think so – but it's slowly gaining."

I thought for a minute. "Skipper to crew, stand by for trouble – we'll just have to take this fella on. Titch, when I say 'Now', I want you to start firing, and continue firing as long as you can see him. Understand?"

"Wilco."

I could feel the hair on the back of my head prickle as I imagined the fighter opening up.

"Right now," I shouted, while at the same time I slammed the throttles shut, and selected flaps down, dropping the nose slightly at the same time. The whole plane vibrated as Titch's twin Brownings roared away.

"Christ," said John, "it's just swept over us with only a few feet to spare."

"Where is it now?"

"It's banked to starboard and is diving down." "Any sign of damage?"

"No; it all happened so quickly."

"Of course there was damage, Skipper, I was firing straight in to him all the time."

I raised the flaps and opened up the engines to zero boost.

"Wally, can you hear me?"

"Sure thing, Skipper."

"There's about five-tenths cumulus cloud about 500 feet below, I'm going to fly through it."

"Roger."

"And I'm going to do a zigzag course. I'm altering course by 20 degrees to starboard. Do you understand?"

"Roger."

"Every minute I want to fly 40 degrees to port, and then 40 degrees to starboard."

"Roger."

"And I want you to tell me when to alter course."

"Wilco, Skipper."

We carried on like this for an hour, and by then I was beginning to relax.

"I think it would be safe to carry on normally now. Give me a course to steer as soon as you can."

"Wilco, but I would like to take a couple of star shots first."

I noted the slight difference in trim as Wally went back to his table. Over the chart-table was fitted a projector. Switching this on, he found two sets of parallel curves projected on to the chart. If his altitude was 25.5, then he would find the curves marked 25 and 26 and draw a line halfway between the two. After doing the same with his second star reading, he soon had an accurate position plotted.

I turned to John,

"Think it's time you took over."

I unstrapped my safety harness and edged out of the seat, allowing John to take over the controls. Turning, I moved back until

I was standing behind Wally, where I could study the chart and admire his work. Every course that we had flown was neatly drawn. Wally looked up and smiled.

"See: that's our D.R. position, where I thought we were, and that's the correct position by astro, only 3 miles away."

It took a particular form of courage, I thought, to remain at a desk with ruler and pencil while anything could be happening around. I had a quick memory of Roy before pushing it away. I was proud of Wally's work. Such a difference from my navigator at O.T.U. Then, I had foolishly flown some random courses while looking for a turning point. My navigator did not bother, and so we were shot at over Calais when we should have been over Dover Castle.

"E.T.A. should be in 35 minutes." I nodded and returned to the second pilot's seat. Well done, everyone, I thought, now it was John's turn.

"Right, John, you're in charge – I want you to land and taxi to dispersal."

While I watched, John brought the aircraft into the circuit. He flew downwind about a mile out from the runway at 1,000 feet, lowered the undercarriage and moved the propeller's pitch into fine. He flew on beyond the end of the runway, and when he judged it right he turned across wind and began to descend. He selected "flaps down" and watched to make sure his airspeed did not drop, then at 500 feet he turned in line with the runway. Looking up from his airspeed instrument, he noticed that he could now see the glide-path indicator.

The glide-path indicator was a light at the beginning of the runway that was covered at the top with yellow glass and at the bottom with red glass, while in between there was a narrow strip of green. John could see that it was showing yellow, so he closed the throttles a little until it went green and then red. He opened the engines a little more and was gratified to see it turn to green again, and so he remained calm until the plane swept over the perimeter at about 20 feet. Leaving the engines on, he ran the wheels along the flare-path and only then did he cut the power.

"Well done, John – couldn't have done it better myself."

The intelligence officer listened to our story. Titch was beside himself with excitement.

"But could you identify the aircraft?"

"No, it was dark and there was no moon."

"How did you know it was there, then?"

"I suddenly noticed that a star had disappeared, and then another, and I was sure there was something there."

"Did any of you notice it crash?"

"I was in the astrodome when it flashed right over the top of us. I think it was a single-engined aircraft of some sort. Anyway, it banked away and dived down."

"Was there any sign of a fire?" John shook his head.

"Then we can't tell whether it was damaged."

"Damaged? Of course it was damaged. As soon as I started firing it came racing up at us until I thought it would end up in my gun turret. I didn't have to aim because it was impossible to miss."

"That's as may be. I'll record it as a probable, and if any of our ground troops report wreckage then I'll alter the record." He looked at me.

"You know, sergeant, you're living up to your reputation. You were a sitting duck, the fighter had only to open up and it would have been curtains."

"I'm aware of that sir, but it was not luck, it was because the chap had underestimated the vigilance of Titch here. *He* saved our necks, not my luck."

CHAPTER TEN

# A Refresher Course

A few days later, I was called back to the office. "I've got two pieces of news for you, sergeant."

"I hope it's good news, sir."

"Yes it is, because the first thing is that your promotion has come through. You are now classified as a warrant officer class I."

I looked at the flight commander in surprise. "Thank you. One tends to forget rank here."

"I know what you mean, but perhaps my second bit of news may be more interesting – because your crew are being stood down for a week. All of you are to undergo refresher courses. You, for example, are being sent back to base at Kabrit for a beam approach course. Do you know anything about it?"

"Never heard of it."

"I'm sure you'll enjoy it, and anyway it will be nice to have a real bath. I'm quite envious! Anyway, take your hold-all with your basic kit tomorrow to the guard-room at ten, and you can travel to the station with the mail. Pick up your travel vouchers at the orderly room. Best of luck, and I'll see you next week."

And so once again I found myself sitting beside the corporal i/c mail, but now the atmosphere was different for the corporal was aware of my reputation, and treated me with great respect. I noticed him glancing at the brand-new coat of arms that was badly sewn on to my tunic.

"Will you be gone for long, sir?"

"No – only a week, on a course at Kabrit." "Kabrit. eh? Lucky bugger, I'd give anything to get back there again."

"You never know, you might find yourself back there sooner than you expect."

"Some hope, but stranger things have happened I suppose."

I left him in the concourse of Cairo station, and strolled off to join the noisy throng round the ticket windows. I presented my travel warrant and found that the journey would take about 2 hours. It was quite an experience, for the train was crowded as usual so I sat on my hold-all in the corridor, until it drew in at Kabrit station, where the R.T.O. took it all as a matter of fact.

"You'll find a party going to the airfield; join them, and the coach will take you all the way."

After the dust of the desert, I found the base overwhelming. It was a permanent establishment built around 20 years ago. I found myself in a real room, with a bed, table and chair, and even a little shelf for books. A little way away along a road lined with flower beds was the warrant officer's mess. I had never been in one before, and was thrilled to find that I was waited on by mess servants. There was a bar with real glasses, and even music – although it came from an elderly gramophone, and one record that contained a scratchy version of "The Birth of the Blues".

The station had been taken over by the Americans, so the food was different from what I had expected. Huge pork chops an inch thick and white fluffy bread, while breakfast was surprising because it consisted of fried bacon and egg, with a pancake smothered in maple syrup on the same plate.

I discovered the theatre that had shows once a week and the cinema that was open every night. There was also a dance at the weekend. I went along and found it reminded me very much of my first dance at home.

Then, I could remember feeling embarrassed, dressed as I was in the uniform of a sailor. I felt more and more scared, and for two pins I would have turned round and walked away; but, gritting my teeth, I opened the door of the Parish Hall. Inside were two ladies sitting at a table. One looked up and smiled,

"Hello, its Bill Bailey isn't it. When will you be going back?"

The other took my sixpence and stamped the back of my hand. I looked at it with surprise.

"That, love, is to allow you to go in and out without paying again. I know what you boys like to do." She laughed and stamped the hand of the girl behind me.

All the chairs had been placed around the room, keeping the floor in the centre empty for dancing. It seemed coated in a white powder, perhaps to reduce slipperiness, and I noticed that the walls were almost covered with notices about the Cadets, the Scouts, and the St. John's Ambulance volunteers. My old teacher was on the stage, fiddling with a gramophone, and a crowd of lads were gathered around a table full of glasses of lemonade, chocolate bars and cakes. In a similar fashion the girls seemed to cling together for support at the other end.

Suddenly the music started and my old mate Archie stubbed out his cigarette.

"Must go, want to dance with Sophie. Do you remember her in our class? She's hot stuff, I can tell you."

He strolled across the floor and soon was dancing around with … but surely that wasn't Sophie! – for this girl was blonde, fat, and had startling pillar-box red lips. I looked away to study all the other dancers and felt reassured, for I could see that many of the chaps were just strutting around with no sense of rhythm at all. Yet it was strange to see so many of my old classmates after all this time, and I wondered if any of them remembered me. And then the hair on the back of my neck prickled.

"Take your partners for a ladies-excuse-me waltz." I decided to dive in, so I nervously I edged round the room to a girl who had been in my class.

"May I have this dance?" I asked politely.

Maggie chuckled, "There's no need to be so polite," she said, "Now let's show 'em."

I was relieved to discover that I quite enjoyed it.

The French chalk on the floor made it easy to make the steps, and Maggie was a good dancer. With her help, we gyrated rhythmically around the room. In fact, I was so wrapped up in the dance that at first I felt irritated when someone touched Maggie on the shoulder, causing her to turn away – leaving me face-to-face with Peggy.

This sudden confrontation made my heart miss a beat. No longer was she a schoolgirl with her hair done up and wearing glasses, but an attractive young lady smiling at me. Somehow she looked much more grown up, with a hint of make-up and lipstick.

"Well, well, Billy – you didn't tell me you could dance." She placed her hand lightly on my shoulder, and timidly I placed my arm around her waist. Together, listening to the music, we danced away. I had enjoyed dancing with Maggie, but this was in a different league altogether. As I danced I was conscious of her perfume, of her hair tumbling over her face and the softness of her body. Enjoying the experience, we danced in silence, each of us absorbed in the other, until the music ended.

"Thank you," Peggy said. "Shall we dance again later?"

I nodded, "I would like that". I took her hand and guided her back to her seat.

Having had the first dance with Peggy, I thought I should dance with some of the other girls. Although I enjoyed it, it was never the same, so after a while I strolled over to the refreshment table and bought a glass of lemonade. I stood near the wall idly reading the display of Brownies' work when I felt someone touch me on the shoulder.

"Bill Bailey, isn't it? Do you remember me?"

I looked round and found it to be the peroxide blonde that had been Archie's partner.

"Of course," I said, "It's Sophie Turner."

"Clever boy. I didn't think you would recognise me. It's a long time since we were in Standard Seven."

I looked at her and decided that she seemed a good sort, even if she was not my type. "Tell you the truth, I wouldn't have known you if it hadn't been for Archie telling me who you were."

She nodded. "It's the hair, you see, it makes me look more glamorous."

I agreed, although secretly I thought it hideous. "What are you doing now?"

"Secretarial at the Poly. Next year will be my last year." The gramophone started up again.

"How about dancing with me. It's a quick-step, and I'm sure you can do it."

I nodded, and the two of us joined the throng on the floor.

I found it hard work, for she was a heavy dancer and seemed to need pushing around the floor. By the time we had finished, I felt exhausted.

"It's getting hot in here," she said, "Suppose we go outside for some fresh air?"

She took my hand and led me past the lady at the door. At the time, I was so innocent that I really thought we were going outside for some air; but Sophie had different ideas, as any boy there could have told me.

Along the side of the hall grew a tall, dense privet hedge that afforded a dark narrow gap between it and the wall. Sophie pulled me into the gap, taking the place of a couple that had just left. She turned towards me and flung her arms around my neck.

"Now let's have a snog," she said. I soon found myself kissing the generous red lips in a passionate lengthy embrace. She pushed her body tight against me and I was aware of the huge breasts squashed against my chest. Rhythmically she rubbed her body between my legs, and I could feel myself being aroused in spite of my distaste for the girl. Suddenly she pulled herself away, tossed her locks and brushed herself down.

"That was nice. See you, Billy." She grinned, "Better go to the loo to wipe the lipstick off."

She was gone in a flash and I, bemused by everything, hurried to the gents. I looked at myself in the mirror and was annoyed to see the smear over my mouth. If Peggy saw that... And then I thought: Peggy, did she see me leave with Sophie? Hell, why did I allow myself to be pulled out? Nothing for it – must face the music. I was relieved to find her dancing with someone else. Why, it was that drip Tubby Hansom. He had been a bit of a gang leader at school. As his mother ran the sweet shop, he always had an endless supply to curry favour with the other boys.

It was getting close to the end, so I edged my way to where Peggy would return. The dance ended and soon she was standing by my side.

"Have you enjoyed your first dance?" she queried. "Very much."

"You seem to have made yourself popular." I looked at her sharply. What did she mean by that? Then Mr Taylor called out,

"Take your partners for the last waltz." I turned to Peggy, but before I could say anything Tubby was standing in front of her.

"Come on, girl, let's dance."

Peggy looked at him, smiled sweetly and said, "I'm sorry, I've already promised it to Billy," then, taking me by the hand, led me on to the floor leaving a furious Tubby glaring after us. We danced, oblivious to everyone else, until the end when I said, "May I be allowed to escort you home?"

Peggy laughed, "Don't be so old-fashioned. Of course, wait for me outside the cloakroom while I get my coat."

I stood to one side as girls rushed in and out talking excitedly, until Peggy came out with a scarf over her hair. She took my arm and we walked out of the hall. By this time it was quite dark, the only light coming from the uncurtained windows of the hall; and so we were surprised by a bunch of boys blocking the path. As they got nearer I could see that the ring-leader was the ginger-haired Tubby Hansom, and I felt my mouth go dry because it was obvious that I was in for trouble.

"Bailey, you've taken my girl. Hop it, go on, hop it."

"I beg your pardon?" I replied.

There was a roar of laughter from the gang.

"Listen to him, I beg your pardon." Tubby said in mimicry. "Just because you're dressed in a poncy uniform you think you can get away with it. Peggy's my girl, so run before I knock your block off."

I looked at Peggy and saw her give a little shake of her head, so I dropped my arm and took a step forward. Tubby took this as a challenge and sailed forward, his arms flying in all directions, until I found myself engaged in a rough-house composed of boxing, wrestling and a little kicking. It reminded me of my first round in the boxing tournament, but this time I was well prepared. I smothered his blows as best I could, and after a few minutes managed to get him an arm's distance away. I had an inch or two longer reach, and so Tubby was left waving his arms in what he thought was a threatening posture.

I was now quite confident and smiled at his helplessness, watching for an opportunity. I brought my right arm back and dealt him a blow that sounded like a pistol shot. I pulled him a little towards me and then with all my force pushed him away, making him fall backward to lay on the ground holding his face and crying with pain. All the other boys stood around, grinning.

"I'll pay you back for this if it's the last thing I do."

I ignored him and turned to Peggy. "Let's go," I said.

We walked in silence to the corner, while Peggy was flabbergasted at my actions. Finally she broke the silence. Looking up at me, she said, "I don't know what to say, Bill, If I hadn't seen it with my own eyes I would never have believed it."

"I was surprised myself."

"I was going to ask you if you enjoyed your first dance."

"It's been more eventful than I expected, but yes, I think I enjoyed it."

Peggy stopped at a white garden gate.

"I live here," she said. She stood and looked at me. I stood and looked at her, and then, remembering Sophie, I hesitatingly placed my arms around her. She timidly turned up her face and slowly I bent forward and lightly touched my lips on hers.

Here in the mess, the dance was pretty much the same as all staff dances; however, whether it was my memories or something else, I did find a W.A.A.F. who reminded me very much of Peggy back at home. But what made the base really astonishing to me was that it seemed to be beside the sea. I found I could walk along the beach and watch the sun glittering on the water and big birds like pelicans diving and coming up with fish. In fact it was not on the sea – the station was built on the shore of the Bitter Lakes that formed part of the Suez Canal.

The course began the next day, and I found myself sitting in a classroom with eleven other pilots. I watched as a flight lieutenant switched on an overhead projector.

"Gentlemen," he began, "My name is Simpson and I'm in charge of this course. Today I want to introduce you to the radio beam approach system." He displayed his first transparency: "As you can see, the system is based on two radio transmitters both operating on the same frequency. They are situated either side of the runway. This one transmits a series of long pulses of sound, while this one on the other side transmits short bursts. It is so arranged that the short pulses exactly fill the gaps between the long pulses, and as the signals overlap slightly it means that when you are over the runway all you hear is a continuous note. If you fly to one side or the other, then the note begins to warble.

There are two other transmitters, but your instructors will tell you all about them later."

The aircraft were standard Wellingtons, but what caught my eye was the windscreen, as I had never seen an aircraft fitted with brown windows. It was as if the plane was wearing sunglasses. However, when we started flying all was revealed. The windscreen, I was told, was covered with a polarising film. I was given sun-glasses to wear and to my surprise discovered that although I could read the instruments, outside everything was black. This was due to the glasses having a different angle of polarity to the windows.

We took off with my instructor flying. We flew across the beam a number of times, so that I could see how the warbling note and steady note coincided with the runway. I was shown the landing procedure by flying downwind over the runway. I noticed that at the end there was a radio beacon called the inner marker beacon that transmitted a high-pitched note over a very confined space. My instructor told me that it was only 100 feet in circumference at 1,000 feet.

"This," said my mentor, "is where you must lower the under-carriage. When you hear the outer marker, a deep note, then you must turn right 30 degrees and fly for one minute, and then do a precise rate one turn to the left. If your flying is accurate you will find that this will bring you right into the beam in the opposite direction." While he was talking, he demonstrated as I listened into my earphones at the signal.

"Right," my teacher went on, "Now we'll try a landing." He flew back over the inner marker and lowered the wheels.

"That's the outer marker, so we do our turn but this time reduce height to 500 feet. You must not go lower until you hear the outer marker a second time. There it is – so down we go, pitch, flaps, keep in the beam and drop down to 20 feet. There's the inner marker ... and over the perimeter and down with a perfect landing."

He turned and smiled. "Care to have a go?"

It all seemed quite straightforward to me, but when I wore my glasses and found myself landing blind it was a different thing entirely. It took a lot of nerve to drop down from the outer marker to the height of a large tree.

That was the reason for the course. Over and over again, day after day, we repeated the exercise until I found I had complete confidence and could land as easily blind as sighted.

It was the last day of the course. I took off in the normal way, but before the plane was airborne it started veering to the side. Immediately my teacher slammed the throttles shut.

"Keep it straight, man." The plane sped on, slowly losing speed, but the runway was not long enough. The inevitable happened and we bumped over the perimeter, demolishing a small rock wall and ending up in the water of the Bitter Lake some 15 feet out from the shore. We were in no danger, but we escaped by opening the astrodome and scrambling on to the wing. There, we edged along to the tip before dropping into the water, which I found quite warm and so quite enjoyed the experience. We got together to check that we were all O.K., and then joined a little crowd that had gathered to share our discomfort. They all seemed to be staring at the tail, so I looked the same way. I noticed that in the rear turret could be seen the head of a man with the water up to his chin.

While I was studying this, a jeep drove up containing the station engineer and the chief gunnery officer. The latter looked at the plane and let off a stream of profanities.

"How many times have I told rear gunners to always have their turret turned to the side on take off? It's to avoid things like this. To escape then, they only have to jettison the doors and fall out." He turned to the station engineer.

"How long will it take you to tow it out?"

"About 2 hours."

"Then leave the so-and-so in there. It will teach him a lesson."

My instructor looked at me with raised eyebrows, for we both knew that the man in the rear turret was the flight mechanic who had asked if he could come for the ride.

CHAPTER ELEVEN

# We Change Airfields

I thought how marvellous it was to meet up with my crew once more. I had not realised what a strong bond existed, for we were not highly sociable – in fact we all tended to keep ourselves to ourselves; but our shared experiences had forged us together as one unit.

We sat on our beds chatting away when Wally said,

"By the way, I did hear that we have all to report for briefing at ten tomorrow morning."

I gazed at him in astonishment.

"Do you mean that we shall be flying ops during the day?"

"No idea, I'm just telling you what I heard in the nav department."

"If it's true," said John, "it would be quite interesting."

But it wasn't, as we all found out when we reported for briefing.

"As you know we are beating the enemy back, and so the complete squadron is moving to an advanced landing ground 150 miles to the east. Pack up all your kit and take it to your aircraft, and be ready to take off from 14:00 hours. Planes will take off alphabetically at 30-second intervals. Fly at 2,000 feet and follow the coast. Navigators can collect the position later."

We looked at each other.

"Can't be worse than this dump," said Tommy. "I'm afraid there will only be a packed meal, as most of the ground staff has already left."

It wasn't pleasant lugging all our kit around in the hot sun, but by 1 o'clock we had stowed it all away. Soon it was time to leave and John taxied the plane onto the runway. I sat by his side and felt that I was going to enjoy this. Two thousand feet meant that I could look down and enjoy the scenery.

However, it was not all pleasure: the scrub, sand, and rocky outcrops brought back unpleasant memories. I began to study the coastline with its occasional white fishing village, and the coast road that I could see was full of traffic moving in our direction.

We had been flying for an hour when my attention was drawn back to the desert. It was obvious that a terrific tank battle had been fought just there. The area had been swept for bodies but was otherwise untouched, and I wondered if a radio van like mine was down there somewhere.

"E.T.A. in 5 minutes," called Wally, who was map-reading from the astrodome.

It looked very much the same as the airstrip that we had left; and so it was, the only difference being that the tents were Italian. Inside each was a green mosquito net that could be zipped up at night. Not that there were any mosquitoes there, but the nets were quite useful as a defence against flies. Normally when we did our little bits of laundry, the clothes would be black with flies within seconds, but if they were hung out inside the tent with the net zipped up then they dried comparatively clean.

But it was not the accommodation that had caught my eye. As John was making his approach, I noticed that the desert just over the coast road was littered with junk, and I wondered whether I might be able to find something with which to amuse myself. As soon as we had settled in, I strolled away to see what I could find. Taking care of the continual stream of tank transporters and heavy lorries going by, I crossed the road and started to explore. I hadn't gone far when I noticed a petrol bowser, a small petrol tanker, and as I walked towards it I was aware of a strong smell. I then noticed that it was leaking. Round the side I noticed a valve that seemed to be in better condition than the rest. I tried it and found that it opened quite easily, and not only that but underneath the tank was a clean jerrycan. Obviously someone else had had the same idea; however, it did mean that if anything workable was left, then there would be an ample supply of fuel. I was out of luck, for everything I checked was far too damaged to be of any use. Then I noticed, half buried in sand, a motorbike. I scraped some sand away, and to my inexpert eye it looked workable. So I returned to camp turning over in my mind what to do.

The crew had not noticed my absence, and so I sat on my bed and started adjusting the straps on my helmet.

"By the way," I said, "Have any of you had any experience with motorbikes?"

Titch, the rear-gunner, looked up. "Yeah, worked for some time in a garage repairing the things. Why do you ask?"

"Well, as a matter of fact I think I have found one."

The crew looked at me in astonishment. "Where?" "Just the other side of the road. How about it, Titch – will you come and look it over?"

"*Will* I come and look it over! Try and stop me. Do we go now?"

"Why not?"

We all erupted out of the tent and, avoiding the traffic, dashed across the road.

"My, my," said Titch, as together we had managed to stand the machine upright. "It's a 1,000 c.c. opposed-piston B.M.W. What a beauty."

"Will it work, do you think?"

"Let's try." He shook the tank. "Yes, it's about half full of juice … Oh dear, that's the reason."

"The reason for what?"

"For it being abandoned." He picked up a broken cable that dangled from the handlebars.

"It's the clutch cable, you can't get anywhere without that."

"Can it be repaired?"

"Not without the proper tools."

I felt disappointed. "Will the engine go, do you think?"

"What's the point? – you can't go anywhere. Still we'll have a go."

He bent over the tank and turned the petrol on, then cleaned the sand away from the coiled copper pipe that led to the carburettor. We watched as he pressed the little plunger on the top, and were thrilled when suddenly petrol gushed out.

"Now let's have a go." Titch pushed hard on the kick-start and after one or two goes the engine burst into life. He looked up and grinned.

"There you are – nothing wrong but the cable." Sitting astride the machine, he revved the engine with the throttle control, while the rest of us admired the full-throated roar.

"Trouble is, you see, I can't get it into gear. I'll show you, stand aside."

He took hold of the gear lever and, having reduced the revs to a tick-over, suddenly jammed the gear lever forward. There was a frightening grating but he persisted, and then suddenly with a click the machine jerked and started moving slowly forward. We gave whoops of glee as Titch increased the power and started moving round and round in circles.

We all wanted to have a go and under Titch's instruction we soon became expert, but it was not long before we became restless at only being able to use bottom gear.

"What's this other control, Titch?"

"That's a valve lifter that's used to stop the engine. Without it you would have to switch off the petrol and then wait for the carb to empty, but ... Hang on; you've given me an idea."

He rode away, but this time increased speed to almost its maximum. Then there was a new noise, a click, and away he went in another gear. Shouting with delight and waving an arm, he returned.

"We've cracked it!" he shouted. He brought the bike to a halt and we all gathered round.

"Let me try to explain. To make a clutch-less change, the speed of the bike, and the speed of the engine, must be more or less the same. This bike has enough power to go away from stop without a clutch. Now, to get the bike going over the ground fast in bottom gear, the engine has to go very fast. If you wanted to go at the same speed in a different gear, then the engine must slow down without the bike slowing down. You can do that with the valve lifter. As soon as you operate that, then the engine will slow down and so when you think the engine is going at the right speed, then you change gear. It's easy."

"It doesn't sound easy to me."

"Well, I must admit it's a matter of judgement, but you'll soon get the hang of it."

Feeling very pleased with ourselves, we brought the bike back and parked it outside our tent. From then on all our spare time was taken up with riding or polishing it. We were the envy of the squadron.

Operations were pretty routine, for we had to harass the retreating enemy by bombing tanks and transport throughout the night. Each squadron was given 2 hours when they were responsible for this chore. We took off with a full bomb load of 250-pound bombs, and each bomb had a 12-inch iron rod, ending in a metal button, welded to the nose. The idea was to enable the bomb to explode before it buried itself in the sand.

After the first trip we came back with Wally looking miserable.

"What's up?" I asked, "Things went according to plan, didn't they?"

"Well, not exactly. In fact, it was 15 minutes before I could find out where we were and so be able to plot course for home."

"Well, you can't be expected to plot courses *and* lay in the bomb aimer's position at the same time."

"That's just it ... but I only feel happy when I know where we are. I don't like flying around the sky blind. The fact is, we really need two navigators."

I could sympathise with this, for I had been in a similar position myself when training. Then I had an idea.

"Tell you what, Wally – why don't we let John drop the bombs?"

Wally looked at me in astonishment. "But he's a pilot!"

"What does that matter? After all, it's not that it would make much difference. The tanks are not exactly floodlit, and I'm pretty certain the whole thing is a waste of time."

Wally thought about it for a while.

"O.K., it sounds a good idea, but we must keep it quiet or we'll get a good rap over the knuckles."

We planned to allow Wally free rein, and so he would plot a series of courses lasting one minute each, making certain that the whole target area was covered. Then John would remain in the bomb-aimer's position and would drop a bomb whenever a target appeared between the wires of the bomb-sight, while at the same time reporting to Wally so that he could plot its position.

It worked really well, and all the strain was taken from Wally, allowing him to be meticulous in the upkeep of his air-plot.

This worked well for a few days, until Wally and I were called to the flight commander's office. We looked at each other as our hearts sank.

"We're in real trouble now."

When we approached the tent we could hear voices inside, and it certainly seemed that there was some sort of court of enquiry going on. Surely, I thought, it was not as serious as all that. We marched in, stood to attention and saluted. Sitting at the table were three officers we knew, while behind, as immaculate as ever, stood the C.O.

"At ease, men," he said, and stood studying us while I was only too acutely aware of our dusty, scruffy appearance.

"Is this the best we have?"

"Sergeant Simmonds, sir, is the best navigator on the squadron. He never gets lost like some of my navigators. His logs are always correct and he even plots the position of every bomb dropped."

I gave a quick look at Wally, who was having difficulty in keeping a straight face.

"And I can assure you sir," said their flight commander, "that Warrant Officer Bailey is the best skipper in my flight and probably in the whole squadron."

"Very well, then, if you say so – although I would have preferred the responsibility to be taken by officers. Well, must go." He walked to the tent flap as the three officers stood up.

They looked at each other and grinned as they sat down.

"Right now, lads, there's a couple of chairs over there. Pull them up to the table and sit down."

He waited until we had joined the officers around the table.

"Take no notice of the C.O., he's a big snob. Now, lads – we want you to look at this."

He pulled a green file toward him, opened it, and removed two aerial photos which he handed out to us.

"What do you make of this?"

I stared at the picture, which was of a conglomeration of tanks and motor transport.

"Is it the target for tonight?" He handed us another picture. "How about that?"

It was a photograph of an arid rocky landscape with steep escarpments separating craggy outcrops.

"Look carefully at the bottom left corner. Hang on, here's a magnifying glass for each of you."

I studied the bottom of the picture.

"Yes, I see all that transport is parked at the beginning of that cliff."

"Now look carefully, and see if you can see why it's there."

"Is that a road leading through the mountains?"

"Yes. Now, Simmonds – could you drop a bomb on that road?"

"No way, sir."

"Why not?"

"Well, it would be impossible to see at night. Even with the moon being exactly right, it would be too easy to mistake one crag for another."

"How about during the day?" Wally looked up quickly. "During the day?"

"That's what I said."

Wally looked at the photo carefully. "At what height was this taken?"

"Four thousand feet, your bombing height. That's exactly what you would see before you bombed."

"Well, it's possible I suppose; but we always fly at night."

"Not this time."

The flight commander interrupted.

"Bill, the idea is for you to fly X-X-ray with one 4,000-pound bomb. You would have fighter cover at 10,000 feet and would probably not experience much ground defence."

I looked at Wally in astonishment. "What do you think, could you cope?"

"Yes I think so."

"Right then, let's have a bash."

The Navigation Officer stood up. "Right then, Simmonds, if you come with me we'll sort out all the fine details."

As they left the tent, the information officer gathered up his pictures and magnifying glasses while the flight commander studied the man in front of him.

"Do you know where X-ray is?"

"Yes it's in the dispersal near the road."

"Right, it's being fuelled up and bombed up as we speak. I suggest you tell the rest of your crew what's happening and then go over and check the aircraft out. All of you should have a meal and be on board by 1:30 for take-off at 2:00. Is that understood?"

"Yes, sir."

"Off you go, then."

I turned to walk away, then hesitated. I turned and looked at my flight commander.

"Thank you, sir, for what you said about me to the C.O."

"That's all right – just make certain the old codger doesn't have a chance of saying 'I told you so'."

"Wilco, sir." I turned and left the tent.

I sat at the controls watching intently the black-and-white chequered wooden hut that stood at the beginning of the runway. Suddenly, a green Aldis lamp flashed my signal letters.

"O.K. chaps, we're on our way."

I moved the starboard throttle forward, swinging the heavy aircraft round ready for take-off. Then, opening both throttles, I guided the plane as it gained speed along the runway. At take-off speed I lifted the plane off the ground and selected "wheels up".

"Right, Wally – it's all up to you."

"Fine, Skipper – all I want is accurate courses and accurate airspeeds."

"You've got it."

"Start by circling the airfield until you reach 4,000 feet."

"Roger. John, I want you to stay in the astrodome all the way and keep a continuous watch on our fighter cover."

I glanced at him as he sat by my side. John nodded and left his seat and moved as requested.

Things settled down with everyone alert and watchful.

"At 4,000 now."

Wally appeared at my side, a map in his hand.

"Steer 220 degrees."

I nodded and swung the plane around onto the course. Wally watched intently through the windscreen, and as we passed the centre of the field he glanced at his watch.

He sat there sometimes looking at his map and sometimes studying the ground. Suddenly he glanced again at his watch and moved back to his table.

"Navigator to Skipper. I've just got a pinpoint and found that the met wind is 4 miles an hour too strong. Alter course to 223."

"Wilco."

We flew in silence for about half an hour when John said, "Our fighter cover has arrived."

"Good, watch them all the time and let me know if there is any activity."

"Navigator to front gunner. Let me know when you see some rocks and mountains ahead. You should begin to see them any time now."

"I think I can see them now, but there's a bit of cloud."

"Skipper, I want to check on the wind again as I need an accurate drift reading for the bomb-sight. I'm coming down now."

He edged past me and laid himself down in the bomb-aimer's position, studying the ground through the bomb-sight.

"O.K., that's fine – now alter course 60 degrees to the right." He repeated the process, then said, "Last one; alter course 120 degrees to the left."

I waited until Wally got up from the floor and turned the plane back on to its original course, and soon Wally was at my side, map in hand.

"Wind is still the same. Now, listen everyone: we are looking for a pinnacle of rock with two points. Let me know if you see it, for the ground should start rising pretty soon. I reckon the mountain range is just there on the horizon."

It wasn't long before Pinky was calling excitedly from the front turret, "I can see them ahead, and they're stretching right across." It was true, for out of the mist rose a pointed rock, and then more and more, more broken, more irregular as the rocky promontories towered up from the desert floor.

"It's like the bad lands in a cowboy film," shouted Pinky.

Unfortunately we hadn't counted on the cloud that was beginning to bubble up at our height. It was fluffy white fair-weather cumulus, making it appear as though we were flying amongst shining banks of snow, with the ground below appearing and disappearing as we flew through it. I looked at it anxiously. It might be due to orographic uplift, and if that was the case it could get thicker as we approached the target.

"There's a two-pointed rock over there." Wally looked over to the left and nodded.

"That's it," he said, "The road curves round the base of that."

"Get down, then, Wally. I'll fly right over it."

I waited until we had flown past and then, banking over, I flew in a gentle curve until we were about 5 miles away with the rock dead ahead.

"Right – am making a bombing run now."

Wally studied the ground through the bomb-sight.

"Left a little," he cried, "Steady ... Damn, I've lost it in the cloud."

"Don't worry, stay there," I said. "Change the drift for a reciprocal run."

I leant forward and adjusted the direction indicator to read 0, for I had an idea. Keeping an eye on the clock, I flew for exactly one minute, and then turned the plane until the direction indicator read 30; a course I continued to fly for another minute. Then, watching the turn and bank indicator, I turned a perfect rate one turn to a reading of 180.

"Stand by, Wally – any time now."

"Well done, Skip – you're right on the money," shouted Pinky as he saw the two-pointed rock dead ahead.

"Steady again, got it ... left a little ... bomb gone."

We could all feel the plane lift as the bomb disappeared. I banked sharply away to the right.

"Any signs down below, Titch?"

"Suffering suckatabs! – that was one almighty bang."

"Did you see where it landed?"

"Not really, for it soon disappeared in cloud."

"Right," I said, "I'm going to drop 1,000 feet and see if we can get underneath this cloud." I turned the plane and dropped the nose, and soon the snow was scudding just above us. However, in spite of all our observation, all we could see was a cloud of dust.

"John, what's going on upstairs?"

"Fighters are circling around."

"Let's go home. Chalky, send a signal: bomb gone."

CHAPTER TWELVE

# We Move to Malta

It was at briefing that we were told the results of our mission. It was true that the bomb had landed a little to the left of the road, but it was near enough to start a rock slide that had blocked the road completely. We were all so thrilled with the result that we remained up all night playing cards, and so we were ill prepared when the intelligence officer gathered up his papers, saying,

"I have some news for you. After you have had your meals, will you go back to your tent and pack your bags and carry them to the briefing room." He looked around at our astonished faces.

"We are leaving this landing ground in a few hours."

There was an outburst: "Where for?" – "What about our sleep? – we've been up all night, you know".

"You will be told at briefing, which will be at 9:00 hours." He looked at his watch. "I'm afraid you haven't got long, better forget your sleep."

There was almost a holiday atmosphere about the camp as people prepared to leave. Bags were filled and accumulated junk placed in piles at the tent entrances, while essential spares were feverishly packed in all the workshops. It was as though we were all going on leave, for no one regretted leaving L.G. 367 with its World War I tents, its rocky outcrops and its gritty tea. The sooner we saw the back of the place, the better. We knew that within a few days of the last aircraft taking off, the tents would be down, the canvas ablution block dismantled, and the isolation of the wind-swept desert would once again be restored.

Together we half-humped, half-dragged our kit to the briefing room and then joined the other air-crews thronging the marquee.

All tiredness was forgotten as we swapped rumours about our future home. Some thought we were going back to Kabrit, others thought Tripoli; while some, the optimists, believed the squadron had been ordered back to the U.K. As it turned out, we were all wrong: we were told that we were heading for Malta. The usual rigmarole was carried out in a perfunctory way, with the wireless operators being given lists of call-signs and radio frequencies while navigators were issued with fresh maps. "Anyway," said one, "it'll make a change to be flying during the day."

Soon the plane was loaded with the kit-bags and stores, while the three mechanics stood nervously around, for this time they were flying too.

"Come on, you fellas," I cried, "you'll have to sit on top of the stores amidships." The entire centre section was packed high with kitbags, crates of sparking plugs, and tins of potatoes, and the three mechanics clambered up to recline at length like Cleopatra. Titch had been packed into his rear turret earlier, and now the mountain of luggage cut him off from the rest.

"Ready, everyone?" I said, "Imperial Airways flight to Malta about to take off'. I lifted the plane off and, banking to the left, did a climbing turn before heading off over the sparkling sea.

The mechanics peered eagerly out of the little piece of window that they could use, to see the last of the sweaty desert, while Wally worked busily away on a course for Malta and Chalky twiddled with his coloured knobs setting up the frequencies for the Malta area.

"I'm riding along on the crest of a wave," warbled Pinky, enjoying the sun in the front turret.

"I didn't know you were a Boy Scout," interrupted Titch.

"Oh, yes – I was a patrol leader and had three badges."

"You know what this Malta business means, don't you? It means wine, women and song, my boy, that's what it means."

We hadn't thought of it before, but it was certainly true that Malta had been civilised for centuries and would be quite a change from the desert. Gradually the sun permeated the aircraft, and the night on ops began to take its toll.

"Wally, Chalky here. Look, don't worry and make heavy weather of the navigation, for it's just plain sailing and you're probably asleep on your feet right now. Just carry on with this course and then I will get you a series of Q.D.M.s and then we'll fly those until Malta appears."

A Q.D.M. was a signal that read "What is the course to reach you?". To receive it, Chalky had to hold his key down for 30 seconds. During that time two radio stations in Malta would take bearings and pass them to a third station. There they would plot the plane's position and radio a course to steer.

Much against his better judgment, Wally agreed to this because he was really asleep on his feet. In fact we were all feeling dozy. John looked at me.

"You look pretty shattered – would you like me to take over?" I felt I had no choice: I knew that I was feeling very, very tired, for the last 24 hours without sleep was the last straw. I went back with the fitters and lounged on a pile of kitbags, where the sun shone through the astrodome, and the vibration of the aircraft soon had me fast asleep. I was woken by the cries of John ringing in my ears.

"Second Pilot to Captain, Second Pilot to Captain, can you hear me?"

"Yes, I can hear you now – I was asleep."

"I've been following a Q.D.M. as Chalky suggested, and Malta is right ahead."

"O.K. I'll come up." As we approached I could make out the clusters of white roofed houses and the beaches, clean between the rocky crags. Almost the whole of the island had been laid out with a gigantic runway, and landing seemed to hold no problems.

"Happy about landing, John?"

"Sure." I strapped myself into the seat alongside and relaxed while John brought the aircraft slowly and safely down to 1,000 feet. I could see down below the fishing boats pulled up upon the sand, and the figures crouched over the festooned nets. Interesting, I thought that we were the first to arrive. As we did a dummy run over the runway I tried to find another Wellington, but the field seemed empty of all traffic. Every available vantage spot in the aircraft was crammed as we studied the island that was soon to be our home. Wally couldn't push his way to a window, so just sat in his navigator's position, amused at the excited comments of the fitters and the gunners.

He might just as well pack away his gear, for there was no doubt that views of the island from the air would soon be only too familiar. Methodically and efficiently, John brought the plane down, and even I realised that it could not be faulted. The wheels touched and the plane rumbled along the runway without a single bounce. I gazed around in anticipation trying to find out where we would have to taxi, when I realised that something was wrong. It had seemed strange at the time that no other planes could be seen, for surely if Malta was so important then it should be packed with traffic; but the worry bell did not ring until we were coursing along the runway with our tail high.

I stared out of the side window at some motor transport parked between the hangers. There was something familiar and yet strange about them. As I watched, they began to drive towards us – and then I understood, for they were the same colour as my old wireless van and the men were steel-helmeted soldiers.

"Overshoot, quick!" I shouted. John was startled, and he stared ahead and concentrated upon keeping the plane straight while I watched the airspeed slowly, oh so slowly, creep up while the end of the runway approached with breathtaking speed. The engines roared and the plane vibrated as it strained to overcome the drag of the flaps, Seventy, eighty … there was not a chance of coming unstuck at 95, and half the runway had gone. I sat staring, mesmerised by the innocent little windmill that was lazily rotating its canvas sails waiting for us to arrive.

John gripped the control column and then suddenly pulled it back, making the aircraft stagger into the air … until, from about 15 feet, it sank back on to the last few feet of runway. I could feel the hydraulic undercarriage sink as it took the weight, then I could feel the thrust upwards as once again the wheels established themselves, so bouncing the plane into the air. Thirty feet it bounced, hesitated … and then began to sink. John whipped up the wheels and closed his eyes, waiting for the crash. The runway was 50 or 60 feet above the sea; and so, roaring and complaining, the aircraft sank below the level of the runway before holding its height and then began to slowly climb.

"Christ," shouted Pinky, "my turret is all splashed with water." No one answered; we were all holding our breath and just too stunned to reply. I was the first to recover.

"Weave, man, weave," I shouted and John, obeying without question, banked the plane over from one side to the other.

"They're shooting at us," screamed Titch. "They're Jerries, that's why," I said, gripping my hands hard, as, powerless, I watched John taking off the flap and streamlining the aircraft. He was too busy to ask the questions that were flying through his mind, but nevertheless managed to look at me for some explanation.

"Don't ask me;" I replied, "but that can't be Malta."

"What do we do now?"

"What the hell's gone wrong?" queried Wally.

"Damned if I know," I answered, "Come here and have a look."

With his hands full of maps he clambered into the cockpit and one glance was enough. "That's not Malta, it's far too small."

"Where the hell is it, then?" Wally studied his map carefully.

"It must be Pantelleria," he said, "and if so, we are a hell of a long way off track."

"But why did they fire at us?" shouted Pinky.

"Because it's an Italian airbase that's why." John shifted in his seat.

"Let's get out of here," I said. "Give us a course, Wally, quick."

"One three five," Wally replied, "and I'll give you a correct course in a minute."

"Gosh, that's miles out," John said, as he banked over to the new course. He readjusted his grid-ring and his direction indicator.

"Are there any fighters there?"

"I don't know, I didn't even know the place existed."

"We'll know soon – they're probably taking off right this minute to shoot us down."

This was a new thought for me, and I stood up to gaze anxiously around.

"Did you hear that, gunners?" I called, "keep a sharp look out ... and Titch, keep watching behind and high."

But John had another idea. "I reckon we ought to go down very low. We would soon be below their radar, and they would have a difficult task seeing us against the sea."

I agreed to this, for it was a very good idea. Soon we were skimming the waves at a height of about 20 feet. It was always exhilarating, this low flying, thought Pinky with his grandstand view; from the front turret, it's like racing round Brooklands in a high-powered car. I, however, knew of the danger involved, for one slight error on the part of the pilot and we would be straight in, and all the time I had to sit there watching someone else make the errors, the errors that I would be responsible for ... Still, John was flying and now was not the time to upset his concentration.

"I'm going to pull out your intercom jack," I told him, "so that you can concentrate on your flying." John, his eyes screwed up against the glare, stared ahead, his hands controlling the plane with the gentle movements of a ballet dancer. I leaned forward and without getting in my second pilot's way I carefully disconnected him from the system.

"Captain to navigator," I then called, "how the blazes did we get to this place then?"

"I'm not sure I know," said Wally, "to tell you the truth I was dozing, but we shouldn't have been much off the course that should have taken us within sight of Malta. I've been using Q.D.M.s given me by Chalky."

"Chalky, how the hell was the Q.D.M. so far out? Did you confirm the course?"

"Of course I did."

"Then how do you account for it being wrong?"

"It must be those fools at Malta; they must have transmitted the wrong bearing."

"Hello, Bill" called Wally. "Sorry about this, it's all my fault... I've worked out the course and we can stay as we are for the present. We are only about an hour from Malta."

"Do you think we could go up now?"

"That's for you to say, but I reckon 30 minutes from here should see us safe."

"Right, we'll do that then. Do you think that Malta gave us the wrong course?"

"I've been thinking about that. If the bearing was wrong then it could have taken us anywhere, so it's suspicious that we flew slap over there."

"Got it," shouted Chalky over Wally's remarks, "It's Pantelleria, they are using Malta's frequency and call-signs."

"Are you sure?"

"Of course I'm sure. I've just asked for a second Q.D.M. and they gave me a reciprocal of our course. You wait – I'll fix them good and proper."

"Bill, Wally again. I'm sorry I just took it for granted."

"Do you think Chalky's explanation's correct?"

"Almost certain."

I leaned forward and plugged John back into the intercom.

"O.K., up we go to 4,000 feet – we are almost there." I watched as John smoothly opened the throttles to plus one boost to begin climbing away to safety.

Soon I realised that the low flying had taken its toll of John so took over as we approached the island.

There was no doubt about it this time, I thought, for this was Malta right enough. It was so much bigger than that Italian island, and as I gazed down I noticed that it looked like an ivory brooch set in lapis lazuli. The gaping harbour of Valletta was easy to identify; so too was the town clambering upwards on its rocky promontories, and as I looked closer I could see the devastating damage, the roofless houses, and the vast areas of rubble that bore witness to the continual enemy attack. I noticed little flags flying defiantly on the twin towers to the harbour, and as we banked away the rising ground in the centre of the island appeared and the sun gleamed and glinted upon a huge dome in the middle of a fully walled citadel. I could even see right away on the far coast where a little island nestled. As I looked, first at the harbour and then at the little island, I had the fanciful impression that a giant had taken a bite at Malta, leaving the Grand Harbour, and then had spat it out again on the opposite coast.

Wally and John jostled into the cockpit while Chalky filled the astrodome, all of us eager to see the island that was to be our new home.

"It actually looks civilised!" shouted Chalky.

"It should be, it's had a lifestyle of its own back to the days of the Bible," said Wally.

Titch, from his vantage point in the rear turret, called out: "I can see some grass, green grass."

"Damn, I can't see from here," Chalky said, as his view was blocked by the wing. Meanwhile I had joined the circuit and was overwhelmed by the traffic. I could count nine other aircraft; there was nothing for it but to wait my turn. We had plenty of time to study the airfield as we flew round and round. It would be quite a change to land on a runway instead of a flat bit of desert; although this was not necessarily an advantage, for the runway had a strange mottled appearance caused by the efforts of countless soldiers in their daily repairs after the bombing of the night. I noticed the widespread dispersal areas and the stone-blast walls surrounding every single aircraft, and it began to dawn on us that we were in the front line and must be prepared to take a sample of our own medicine. Each of us was wrapped in his own thoughts as I answered the green Aldis and came into land, and soon we were following a slowmoving jeep to our own dispersal pen with its tall rock wall.

An airman with waving arms helped me to swing round, the wing tips inches from the wall, and then when the airman crossed his arms across his chest I switched off both engines. The propellers slowed, twitched and then vibrated backwards and forwards as the dead cylinders reached compression, the whine of the generators fell away, and things were silent. I waited a moment, then, pulling off my helmet, I shouted to my crew.

"We're here, lads, at last. I wonder what's going to happen now."

John opened the hatch at his feet and lowered the ladder to the ground. Soon, the grinning face of the mechanic appeared.

"Welcome to our happy island. You are to unload your gear and wait to be collected."

"Sure thing," said John. "Any chance of some food? We've had nothing to eat since breakfast."

"Eat! We don't eat here, mate. Haven't you heard there's a war on?"

"Funny, funny," replied John, irritably. "Well, if you want us to unload you'd better get out of the way." Stiffly we climbed down, followed by our three passengers. I turned to the corporal and only then did I notice that his face was ashen, while his two mates did not look much better.

"What's up with you three? I thought you'd been sleeping all the way. Don't tell me you've been airsick?"

"Snogger's been sick, but to tell you the truth we're all glad to be back on the ground."

"Not half," said one of the others. "Was shit-scared most of the time. When we came in to land we all thought that we'd arrived, and then to be shot at was too much. That was when Snogger was sick." The man called Snogger shifted his feet uncomfortably,

"It's all very well for you chaps," he said, "being shot at all the time, but I'm not used to it, it's bad for my ulcer."

"Your ulcer!" retorted the corporal, "You've no more an ulcer than I have." The air-crew grinned at each other.

"Now you know what we have to put up with," I said. "By the way, where is Titch?"

The banter ended and I felt my heart beat hard as I remembered the gunfire from below as we had staggered away from Pantelleria. The rear turret was the obvious target. John dashed for the ladder as I walked to the rear of the plane. I had steeled myself for most things, but was surprised and relieved to see a furious Cockney waving and shouting through the perspex.

"Come on you bastards, let me out," he bawled. It dawned upon me that the pile of luggage had trapped Titch in his turret and everyone had forgotten all about him.

I lay on my back in the hot sun gazing up at the rocky blast wall around the plane. Was it really necessary to have them so thick and so high? As I studied it, I was conscious of a claustrophobic feeling, for the wall looked somehow punitive, depriving me of access to life, while the entrance was so small that it seemed impossible to get a Wimpy out. From my position against the kitbags, the wall confined my sight to a small round disc of sky and A-for-Apple, oil-stained and dusty from the journey down.

It seemed somehow as though the whole world existed beyond the circle. Even sounds were muffled and indistinct, like outside traffic dimly audible within a prison cell. A church-bell clanged its solitary discordant note, which was repeated by bell after bell from every point of the compass, each one tolling monotonously and tunelessly like milk churns or oil drums full of stones. I turned my head and studied my crew enviously, for they all seemed asleep, probably exhausted after the flight.

A lorry whipped into the pen, the roar of its engine waking everyone up, and it was the work of a few minutes to pile into the back. Soon we were crowded into a room underneath the control tower.

"Welcome to Malta," said a tired-looking officer with the two rings of a flight lieutenant upon the shoulder of his shirt.

"I am sure you are all hungry, so the first thing is to issue you with a meals card. If you show your paybook to the corporal, he will stamp it and issue your card. Now, you must remember that food is very short on this island, and no meals will be served without a card. Have it with you at all times." He looked down at the piece of paper in his hand.

"You have been given billets in Sliema, and you'll be picked up from the mess and taken there in one hour's time. I think that's all … No: I have a message for the Captain of A-Apple. Will he report to H.Q. as soon as possible." Wally looked at me curiously. What was that, I wondered? Perhaps I was being posted to the U.K.

As we were driven to the mess, I kept thinking about the summons. Would it be back to the U.K.? It was not likely, for I had still a few flying hours to do. I racked my brains, and suddenly had an idea. Perhaps it was a citation. After all, I had been told I was the best skipper on the squadron, and then I had successfully carried out my special mission. The more I thought about it, the more I was sure. It would be nice to be awarded the D.F.M.

## CHAPTER THIRTEEN

# A Call to H.Q.

T he officer was absolutely correct about the meals card. Security was very tight indeed. I pushed my way into the mess – for I knew now that I was hungry – only to be met by an airman at the door. I watched as the man took the card and stabbed it with a pin. I looked at it more closely, and noticed that it had three squares alongside the date. The airman had made a pin-prick in the second square of the day. Three squares, three pinholes, three meals; no possible chance of going round again. It was as the queue was moving slowly towards the hatch that I suddenly remembered that I did not have a knife and fork. I nudged the sergeant ahead.

"Irons," I said, "do we get them at the hatch?"

The sergeant gave me a wan smile. "If you need them, you can get them."

I puzzled over the rather cryptic remark, but all was quickly revealed when at last it was my turn at the hatch – for there were no alternatives: just a plate, a plate containing three cream crackers, two sardines and one foil-wrapped segment of cheese. I looked at it in astonishment.

"Is this all?"

"That's all; you'll get a bigger meal tonight."

As in a dream, I took my lunch to one of the tables.

It was not until we had reached our new billet that I could feel better. We were sharing a two-bedroom flat with four soldiers, with the squaddies in one room and the six of us in the other.

It was true that the flat had seen better days: the mahogany veneer on the doors was beginning to peel off, making a slapping noise every time the doors were moved, but we did have a bathroom between the ten of us, and a lounge, such as it was. It had a sofa with the stuffing coming out of one corner and two armchairs, one of which had a broken leg. There was also a table covered with scratches and rings from countless glasses. Although all six of us were bedded down in the one room, it was still far better than a tent in the desert. No longer was it necessary to shake scorpions from our clothes in the mornings.

I grinned to myself as I watched Chalky trying to tart himself up.

"I wonder if there's a Chinese laundry round here"

I joined him at the window.

"Look down there," he said. I looked down at the street below and the crowds thronging the pavement.

"Quite a change after the desert," Wally said.

"Sure thing, but don't you *see* … Down there, there are women, *talent*; doesn't it do something to you to see them again?" Wally came up to me; it was obvious that he could contain his curiosity no longer.

"This interview at H.Q. Bill, do you know what it's all about?"

I stood up and carefully smoothed my bed.

"I've no idea."

"I'm not so sure," said John, "you've been sitting there as if you're a cat with cream. You must know what it's all about."

"Is there any chance that you are time-expired?" asked Pinky . "You were in this business before us I remember."

"Wish I was, but I've got another 30-odd hours to do, so it can't be that."

"I wish I had only 30 hours to do," John moaned, "Why, that's only about seven ops, you could do that in a month easily." I needed no telling about how long it would take.

"When are you going to find out what it's all about?"

I decided to keep my ideas to myself.

"Frankly I'm as mystified as you, so I reckon there's nothing for it but to get it over and done with."

"Do you know where the H.Q. is?"

"Yes, it's in Valletta apparently, you take one of the boats across the harbour, and then it's underground near the docks."

Pinky looked up. "You're going to Valletta tonight?"

I nodded. "Apparently those office wallahs work until 8:30."

Pinky grinned, "What about it, Titch? Shall we go too?"

"What, to H.Q.? Not likely – I've learned to steer clear of them."

"No, you fool – to Valletta. That's where all the action is, that's where we can find the girls."

Titch thought for a moment. It had to be admitted that he was dog-tired, but it was also true that he had almost forgotten what a girl looked like, and a little female company would be pleasant.

"Well, I did intend to join Wally, Chalky, and John, at the cinema."

"Come on; let's make a night of it. Will you wait for us, Bill, so that we can all go together?"

The ferry was little more than a rowing-boat.

Carefully the three of us stepped into the stern, and sat on the seats expecting the man to ferry us across. He, however, had other ideas, for he intended to get the maximum reward for his efforts, and so he waited until one by one his customers clambered in making the little boat sink lower and lower into the water until the gunwale was less than an inch above the water. Titch watched apprehensively as he leaned against the oars, for any slight lap, much less the wake from another boat, and we would be completely swamped.

"They believe in living dangerously, don't they?" he said.

Pinky looked very uncomfortable "Trouble is, I can't swim," he confessed.

We were dropped at the foot of steps, slippery and slimy with age, and together we clambered up to the square above. At least, it had once been a square; but now, as I looked around, all I could see were the remains of houses and great piles of rubble that bore witness to all the continual air-raids. A church stood stark and lonely in a sea of rubble. A city gate that had stood proud and strong against countless sieges was now ruined, its massive pillars sectioned and tidied away to the side. Further down, I could see the bomb-scarred remains of what was once an elegant theatre or opera house.

"Gosh," said Pinky, "this place has had a bashing. I didn't think it would be like this." He turned to me: "Well, this seems to be the remains of the famous Kingsway. Do you know where you are going?"

"It's supposed to be near the church. Yes, I can see the steps from here."

"O.K. then, old son, we'll say goodbye. You go and wangle your posting while we say hello to the ladies of Valletta."

I descended the treacherous steps into the semidarkness of the underground H.Q. I couldn't help but wonder what all this meant, and I just could not get the idea out of my head that I was due for an award. By the time I had reached the bottom of the steps, I was quite sure that that was the reason for the summons.

As I carefully negotiated the steps, hanging on to the wet and rusty hand-rail, I thought the place was similar to a rather seedy public convenience, and I would not have been surprised to see at the bottom a poster advertising the local V.D. clinic. However, the steps led down into a natural cleft in the rock that formed the foundations of the city. It was this natural rock, with its cracks and fissures, and its rabbit-warren of carved-out cisterns and catacombs, that had helped Valletta to withstand some of the most relentless air attacks in history.

This particular fissure, I found, was about ten feet wide at the bottom, with stone cliffs rising up about thirty feet to the surface. As I gazed up at the damp walls and the occasional fern growing beneath a dripping drain, it reminded me of a holiday I'd taken in Poole before the war; Branksome Chine had been something like this. Here, though, its function was very different, for it made a perfect air-raid shelter, safe from everything but a direct hit. And that was why it was so crowded: crowded with the homeless, with the poor, and with the old. There they sat, huddled against their bundles, cooking with blackened pots over smoky, smelly bonfires, and washing under a water pipe that poured continual rainwater from the rock into a gutter beneath. Some were making an attempt to ply their trade, their tools wedged into chinks in the rock as they repaired shoes or hammered copper – and, here and there, silver – while all the time half-naked children crouched everywhere, their big eyes watching every move.

Embarrassed, and taking care not to stand on something or someone, I edged my way to a wooden barrier and its naval sentry.

"I've been told to report to H.Q," I said.

The sentry grinned. "This is it, mate – who do you want to see?"

I thought for a moment. Should I say I was up for a citation for a D.F.M.? Perhaps that would be being too premature. "I was just told to report to H.Q."

The sentry looked at me. "There are thirty offices in the west wall, and twenty-three in the east. Each outer office leads into other inner offices. Why, if I let you through, you'd be here for the duration finding the right bloke." (I could see the sense in that remark.) "Can't you give me an idea?"

I hesitated; I did not like putting my dreams into words. "It could be R.A.F. Records."

"What's your name?"

"Warrant Officer Bailey."

The sentry stepped into his shelter and I watched him as he phoned around.

"Sorry," he said on his return, "they've never heard of you."

I turned away, uncertain as to what to do, when the phone again rang and the sentry called me back.

"Are you by any chance the captain of a Wellington aircraft A-for-Apple?"

"Yes, that's me."

"Then we do have a message for you. You are to report to the duty signals officer. Come right through, I'll show you where to go."

This was not what I expected at all. What on earth did the signals officer want with me? I knocked at the door and walked in. A civilian typist looked up and smiled.

"Can I help you, sir?"

I explained my errand and looked around as the girl disappeared into an inner office. The place had a vague appearance of a brewer's cellar. I could see that the rooms had been carved out of the rock and then whitewashed. A naked bulb hung from a flex that was festooned from rusty nail to rusty nail across the ceiling, while the only decoration was an Esquire calendar nailed to the opposite wall.

"Come this way, sir. the duty signals officer will see you now."

The signals officer looked up and waited until the two of us were quite alone. From his desk, he studied me intently.

"What is your name, warrant officer?"

"Bailey, sir."

"Are you the captain of Wellington aircraft A-Apple?"

"Yes, sir."

"And you arrived today from the Western Desert?"

"Yes, sir."

"Your signals procedure at your advanced landing ground. I suppose it was a bit sloppy. Procedure not important in the desert, eh?"

For the life of me, I could not see where all these questions were leading.

"No, sir, things were just the same. Of course I left all those things to my wireless operator."

"Of course. You trusted your operator?"

"Certainly, sir, he's one of the best."

The officer leaned back in his chair and I was aware of a steely glint in his eye.

"Would you agree that you are responsible for all that goes on in the aircraft during flight?"

"Of course."

"Then, Bailey," he snapped, "you are responsible for this." He tapped the signals flimsy in front of him.

"You are responsible in wartime for sending signals in plain language without any attempt at coding. Sending messages that could be picked up by the enemy. Destroying completely our confidentiality."

I looked at him in astonishment.

"Come on, Bailey – don't tell me you knew nothing of this?"

"Any messages sent or received were dealt with in the normal manner by the operator."

The lieutenant leaned forward.

"And that's not all. Not only was the message sent in plain language but it was obscene. Do you hear: obscene. How dare you allow filth like this to be sent over the air? Did you know that the MF/DF section here is staffed entirely by girls? Why, your message pretty nearly caused a riot, one girl was in hysterics!"

"I'm sorry, sir" I stammered, "but I have no idea what this is all about. Could I see the message?"

"Here, read it."

"You can stuff your fucking Q.D.M. up your fucking ass," it read. I stared at it with disbelieving eyes. It started in the usual official way, and then written in a girlish hand was the message.

"Can you imagine a young girl receiving that?" The meaning now was clear.

"I can only apologise for my operator, sir. But I think I can understand how it happened."

I told the officer all about Pantelleria.

"So you see," I ended, "it was really for the Italians. Your girl was in a sense eavesdropping upon someone else's signal."

"But it was on our frequency."

"Yes, sir – that was the fact that my operator had forgotten. After all, sir, it nearly caused us all to be prisoners of war."

The naval lieutenant calmed down. In fact, he was beginning to see the funny side of it.

"I can see how it happened. Sorry, warrant officer, to call you over, but we have to check up on things like this. I shall have to write a report, but I'll mention this Italian business and we'll try to get it stopped."

A bell rang and he picked up the phone. I watched his face change as he listened to the message.

"Twenty plus on the plot, thank you." He looked up, "I suggest you find somewhere safe, for we are in for a raid – and a big one, at that."

"Can't I stay here?"

The officer smiled, "I'm afraid not. During a raid we have a red alert with strict security. All strangers must be evacuated ... But don't worry, there are plenty of deep shelters up above."

## CHAPTER FOURTEEN

# An Air Raid

It wasn't until I was walking away from the office that I realised that I had been expecting an award. Of course it was ridiculous, I knew that; and yet ever since that mysterious summons I had gradually built up my expectations, until subconsciously I had begun to believe it. In talking to my friends I had refused to believe in the possibility, and yet all the time I was becoming more and more convinced. But now the bubble had burst and reality had taken the place of fantasy.

As I stumbled up the steps and into the square above, I was grappling with my emotions as a wave of depression overcame me. I held on tight to the hand-rail of yet another flight of steps, and it was not until I had found myself in a cul-de-sac ending in a wrought-iron gate that I began to notice my surroundings. The wrought-iron gate led into a public garden, and so, bending down, I fumbled with the catch until it opened with a squeal of rusty metal. The public convenience inside was surrounded by barbed wire, as if the denial of such fundamental facilities would seriously hamper invading forces; but I ignored this and followed the gravel path leading through the dusty bushes until I came upon a stone parapet overlooking the harbour.

It was the siren on the public conveniences that brought me back to reality with its banshee howl. It was so close that I could see the rotor inside spinning faster and faster as the howl climbed up the scale. Up and down the note went, louder and louder, until I held my ears in an attempt to deaden the sound. And then it whined down to a halt, and I could hear the other sirens all over the city alerting the people to the approaching raid. I stood up and stared into the darkness over the harbour, but all was dark with storm clouds menacing the horizon. The searchlight generator to my left coughed into life, and then with a crackle the arc was made and the whole park was lit with brilliant beams as it swung upward to take its part in quartering the sky.

I looked anxiously to the north as the *crump, crump* of heavy artillery began. I could see the flash of the guns, and could watch the scarlet flowers that began to bloom in the sky. Now I could hear the bombers, their engine note throbbing in the unique Dornier way. The guns around me now began to go mad, the "Chicago pianos" rattling away as though their very existence depended upon it. So this is what it is like to live in an air raid, I thought. It was a strange thing, but all the time I had dropped bombs upon the enemy, I had never before thought about what it was like to be below. At first I was fascinated at the excitement, the noise, the lights and the furious activity, and then suddenly I realised that I should be underground in a shelter. I jumped as an explosion blew a hole in the gravel path, and watched as an incendiary sparked and fizzed with the typical white light of magnesium; then staggered back as it roared away, glowing red in the middle with red sparks of molten metal cascading out to bounce and roll almost to my feet. Then it went out, leaving a crater, some smoke, and the smell of burning tar.

It was then that I realised the danger of my position. The air was full of the screaming of falling bombs, and my ears felt the pressure waves as they exploded nearby. Like a man protecting himself from a violent thunderstorm, I sprinted to the street. The searchlights drew lines upon the sky and coloured tracer streamed across as the guns, hot with exertion, pumped it into the sky. An explosion in the air momentarily lit up the scene as a bomber was hit, bringing it slowly down into the sea in a comet-like parabola.

And then a whine as of an express train filled the air. I threw myself onto my face before the explosion occurred, but I could feel the ground rock at the force of the impact, and then there was a deafness, a stillness. As my hearing returned there was a sound of breaking glass, a rumble of collapsing walls, and the scream of a child in the night. I waited for a moment; then, lifting my head, I slowly rose to my feet. The area was devastated: the buildings around the park had been shattered with one large bomb. Here and there a wall stood alone, but the rest was rubble, smoking and burning like a scene in hell.

The full significance of my position then became clear and I knew in one revealing flash that I was about to die. The tinkling sound, like summer hail upon a laurel bush, was really red-hot shrapnel and I was only too aware that one piece near the brain and I was finished. And yet I couldn't stay there. I picked myself up and ran, away, anywhere ... but I must run. Another screech and I threw myself into a doorway, covering my head with my hands. The explosion deafened me; the pressure wave upset the precarious balance of the unsupported wall and it collapsed as in a Charlie Chaplin film, the door framing my crouching body. Not daring to move, I remained still as the dust settled, my nerves in tatters. And yet there was other human life in that sea of devastation. There were people unable to reach the sanctuary of the shelters: some were trapped under beams and stone, others were cut and bloody from the flying glass – while others, the really unfortunate ones, were lying smashed to pieces by the exploding bombs.

I looked up as I felt a tug on my arm. It was a little boy of about 12, carrying a toddler almost as big as himself with a face that was streaming with blood.

"This way," the boy said, "The shelter is this way." I staggered to my feet and followed him as he picked his way over the smoking ruins. The boy edged his way between two walls leaning over at a crazy angle, stooped beneath an arch, and led the way down the black stone steps. He turned to me. "Don't worry, you'll be quite safe here."

I will never forget that night. The crowded shelter full of people murmuring to themselves, and swaying as they repeated their prayers, the smoking oil lamps dangling from the walls, the screams of the injured in the doorway, and the quiet movements of the first-aid workers who were doing what they could for the injuries around. But it was not long before the sirens sounded again and everyone stood up and made for the door, unconcerned as if they were in a cinema at the end of the big picture, and in a hurry to catch the last bus home. Unconcerned they were, for they knew that it was just an ordinary raid and no doubt there would be another tomorrow.

Our work in Malta was to attack the docks and marshalling yards in Sicily, although there was a cheer when on one occasion the target was Pantelleria. I looked at Chalky, for there was no doubt that other people had also been caught in that trap.

It was, however, hard work, for Sicily was so close that by the time we had reached 4,000 feet we could see the target. It was hardly necessary for Wally to get out a map. And that is what made it such hard work, for we had to do three operations a night, and that meant three take-offs with full bomb load, three times over the target while the Italians tried to blow us out of the sky (or, if you counted photo runs, it was six times), and then three landings. There was no doubt it was doing things the hard way.

The Italians were no slouches at defending themselves, either: Flight Lieutenant De Courcy returned one night with half a wing shot away. There was also little for John to do, because it was the captain's responsibility to take off, land, and fly over the target. Sometimes I thought I would hand over to him, but to tell the truth I was uncertain of my ability with the photoflash.

But, I thought, it was all in a day's work and that night would be the same as the others, touch wood. We were rather lucky to have dispersal near the briefing room, for some crews had to travel miles. As I strolled along the perimeter fence near the dispersal I could see a dusty little limestone house, its flat roof covered with gourds of some description. They were like marrows, only round and yellow. What it was like to live so near aircraft I didn't like to think, but I envied the farmer. I watched as a half-starved chicken scratched around in the dust for a tasty morsel or two, although if she had had any sense in that small brain of hers she would have realised that she had sifted that dust for nutrient many times before.

The first operation was normal, and at debriefing the intelligence officer continued his questions to Wally about where the bombs had dropped. We sat in the trailer having cocoa and sandwiches as the feverish activity outside continued. I sat gazing out of the window and watching the flashes from torches as the mechanics swarmed over the aircraft. I could see that there were three aircraft there: X-X-ray, P-Peter and my own. Soon we would be in the air and another three would take their place, in fact I could see the armourers' tractors bringing out another train of bombs; and I knew that by the time the plane was refuelled we would be ready again for action.

As I left the caravan I was aware of aircraft overhead. Nothing unusual about that, I thought, for after all this was Luqa airfield ... and then I remembered that I had heard that throbbing note of engines unsynchronised before. They were Dorniers! Shouting to my crew, I ran.

"Dive, boys, dive!" I demonstrated by throwing myself full-length into the bottom of the slit trench outside, only to be covered by the rest of the crew.

It was almost the first bomb that scored a direct hit on the petrol bowser. The fireball enveloped the three Wellington aircraft, and everything was a sea of flame. Tracers popping off in the heat sailed in every direction like fireworks in a November bonfire. The aircraft sagged down, their red-hot aluminium slowly melting into pools of molten metal.

Then the bombs exploded, throwing debris into the air as bomb followed bomb. The air was full of the noises of explosions and the whining of ricocheting ammunition. Flight Lieutenant De Courcy could see it was bad as he flew around waiting to land, but what he did not know was the fact that it was his flight that had been caught refuelling.

Stunned, we pulled ourselves to our feet and looked around in amazement; for nothing was left but pools of smoking metal.

## CHAPTER FIFTEEN

# Hospital

The raid caused the bombing programme to be seriously disrupted. For a few days we had to report to the briefing room only to be sent away again until the next day. The boys were grateful for the rest, and while Pinky and Titch spent their time in Valletta, the others became interested in fishing. However, for the last two days I had been feeling out of sorts, with a headache.

"I won't come with you today, lads – I've got a bit of a headache."

I lay back on my bed and closed my eyes. It was rather nice to be on my own for a change, but as the time went on my head became worse until I decided to pay a visit to sick-bay. When I stood up my head throbbed, and throbbed, and by this time I was feeling bad. It was so hot, at least I thought it was, and perspiration streamed off me as I staggered along the street. It seemed such a long way; I was beginning to think this intense heat was more than I could bear, and that I must go home.

I fell against the door and collapsed into the room.

The doctor who was sitting at a desk looked up in astonishment. He stood and helped me up.

"Whatever's up with you?"

"Home, plane, travel warrant," I murmured.

The doctor helped me onto the couch, placed a thermometer into my mouth and took my pulse; then, reading the thermometer, his face changed.

"Hammond, Jones," he shouted, "Here, quick."

Two orderlies appeared.

"Hammond, get a bowl of cold water and raid the fridge for every ice-cube you can find and flannels. If we don't get this man's temperature down fast, he may have brain damage. Jones, help me get him undressed." But I knew nothing of this, for I had slipped into unconsciousness.

Suddenly I came to, as a sharp pain travelled from my face, down my body to my groin, causing me to scream. I opened my eyes to find that the two orderlies were washing me in ice water. It was almost unbearable; and yet, as they went on, I found it quite pleasant. The doctor had placed a thermometer under my arm. When he next read it, he said, "Thank goodness. What's your name, warrant officer?"

"Bailey."

"And where are you now?"

"In Malta."

He held up a paper booklet. "Do you know what this is?"

I studied it. "I think it is my pay-book."

"Good. You don't seem to have suffered any damage. Now, when you came in here your temperature was higher than anything I've ever seen, but now it's down to a fairly safe point. I've sent for an ambulance to take you to hospital, and they will get you back to normal in no time."

I did not remember much of that journey, for I slept most of the way. I was soon lying on a bed with a fan playing upon my body.

It was a recurrence of malaria, they said, and told me they would have me back to normal in about 3 weeks. This turned out to be true, for I made rapid progress and was ready for an air-crew medical almost exactly on time.

"Fine, Bailey," the doctor said, "You are as good as new. I am going to discharge you, but you will have to report to Postings to tell them you are fit for flying. I have a transport going to Sliema this afternoon for stores, and you can travel back to your billet in that."

It was not until I had jumped down from the lorry that I realised how much I had missed my gang. I had no doubt that in my absence John had made an excellent skipper, but it would be nice to take over the controls again.

"I'm back," I shouted as I bounded into our room, and then stopped dead as I looked around. In the corner was a bed carrying all my kit, but apart from that all the other beds were empty and stripped. There was not a sign that my crew had ever been there at all. I turned and entered the soldiers' room and found one squaddy sitting on his bed writing a letter. The soldier looked up.

"So you're back. Are you O.K. now?"

"Yes, thanks – but where is everyone?"

"Were you not told? The squadron was moved away."

"Away?"

"Yeah, too much damage to the planes here and so they've gone to somewhere safe. By the way, your observer chap."

"Wally?"

"Yeah, that's him. He asked us to keep an eye on your kit until you got back."

I turned and surveyed the empty room. It had only just begun to sink in. I had been left alone in Malta knowing nobody, and completely isolated. As in a dream, I went down the stairs and decided to walk along the edge of the harbour. I watched the sun glistening on the water and the many-coloured fishing boats bobbing up and down while the fishermen mended their nets. Perhaps the hospital had known something, for it seemed strange to ask me to report to H.Q. Fancy letting me stay in hospital without telling me! I did not blame my crew, because it had probably come as a shock to them. I grinned to myself as I thought of the comments no doubt made by Pinky and Titch at having to leave their girlfriends behind; but I had never realised until now how much I needed their support. They were always ready to take my advice and obey my requests, and now I had found that they had really been supporting me. I felt completely undecided as to what to do. Should I go across to Valletta and visit the Union Jack club, or should I stay there? In my mind, I thought of what Wally would say. "You've got time to waste – why not go to the cinema?"

This I did – but it was just not the same, queuing on my own and sitting on my own. It did, however, help to waste the time.

As I walked down the steps towards H.Q., I had an idea that perhaps I was being sent back to the U.K., but I dismissed it because I was not going to mislead myself again. I was prepared for anything; and yet I was still surprised when the clerk said that I had been posted to Fighter Command.

"But I fly Wellington bombers."

"Can't help that, chum, it says Fighter Command here, and you must report to Fighter Control right away. It's down there – third door on the left."

Feeling dazed, I tapped on the door and went in.

Sitting inside was a W.A.A.F. who looked up and smiled.

"Warrant Officer Bailey. I was told to report here."

"That's right," she said, and stood up to leave the room by an inner door. A little later, she returned,

"The Chief Controller will see you now."

She led me along a corridor that had been carved out of the rock, tapped on a door and said, "Warrant Officer Bailey, sir."

I entered the room, stood to attention and saluted.

The Squadron Leader standing by the wall studied me carefully and then, as if satisfied, said, "Relax, Mr. Bailey, and take a seat."

He looked at me, and smiled. "I expect you are a little bewildered."

"Yes, sir."

"Let me put you in the picture. Here you can see a large map of Malta. It is divided into six large areas. Here is Luqa, with which you are very familiar. Now, over here," and he pointed to a place on the western coast, "is a disused airstrip called Qrendi. I have decided to recommission that strip, and I want you to be the airfield controller."

"But I know nothing about the work, sir."

"Don't worry, you'll be shown what to do later but now I want to tell you the overall position. In 2 days' time, a squadron of Spitfires will be arriving; and they will be operating from your airstrip. The pilots and the ground crews will be billeted in Rabat and will arrive by coach every morning. They will leave in the same way at 18:00 hours at night. You will be responsible for all the traffic during the day. Is that all right?"

"But I know nothing of ground control."

"Never mind, you will be instructed before you are left. Oh … and another thing: after the crews have left, you will lay out a flare-path so that in case of emergency you can bring the aircraft down. Now, that means, I'm afraid, that you will be on call for 24 hours a day. It seems a lot, I know, but the chances of you being called upon are very remote." He looked down at a paper on his desk.

"Now, the squadron commander will be given instructions to organise a rota of pilots to relieve you for meal breaks, and another for Wednesdays. Wednesday will be your day off, and to allow you to leave the field I am organising an emergency flare-path for Wednesdays at Takhali." My head was spinning at all these instructions.

"I've got Samantha to type out all these orders so that you can study them tonight. Now, on the bottom of the sheet are some details underlined. It is vital that these are carried out to the letter. At 9 o'clock you must be in the control tower, where you will contact the duty controller by V.H.F., and then when the flare-path has been laid you will contact the duty controller by telephone from your quarters. Is that clear?"

"Will I be shown what to do?"

"Yes, I'd forgotten that. Now, an experienced controller from Luqa will pick you up from your billet in Sliema at 9:00 tomorrow. He will take you out to Qrendi, show you your quarters, the control tower and everything, and will go into your work in detail. So that's all, Bailey, but I would like to tell you that you are a vital cog in the defence of the island."

"Would you tell me, sir, what's happened to my squadron?"

"Yes, all bomber squadrons have been withdrawn from the island until we have air superiority – then perhaps they will be back. So you see, if you want your friends back, the best you can do is help sweep the enemy from our skies. That will be all … and the best of luck."

Bewildered and with my head spinning, I turned and left the room.

## CHAPTER SIXTEEN

# My New Job

The senior controller was true to his word: next day, I was tying up the last of my kit when there was a little tap on the door. "Warrant Officer Bailey?"

"That's me."

"Welcome to the ancient order of traffic controllers."

I studied the little man who was grinning at me from the door. He was short, bald, with large goldrimmed glasses. On his chest he wore World War I medals, on his shoulder, the one ring of a flying officer.

"Thompson's the name."

"Bill Bailey."

"Call me Baldy, everyone else does. Right, let me help you with your kit – your transport is outside."

Together we humped the kitbags down the stairs, and tossed them on top of a number of containers like paint drums that were loaded on the back of an open-top jeep.

Baldy sat in the driver's seat and I sat by his side. "We'd better do this first, before I forget." Baldy fished around in the glove compartment and brought out an official-looking form. "Just sign at the bottom, will you."

"What is it?"

"You're just signing for the transport, that's all."

"What transport?"

"This jeep. It is now officially yours. It comes with the job and you'll need it to lay out the flare-path."

I was astounded, "But," I said, "I can't drive." Baldy looked at me in astonishment. "You can't drive?"

I nodded. A slow grin creased Baldy's face.

"How did you think you were going to lay out all these lamps here? – by walking from one end of the runway to the other with a handcart?"

"No one asked me whether I could drive or not."

"The only thing I can say, son, is I hope you are a quick learner."

Baldy switched on the ignition and pulled the jeep into the main traffic stream. Soon we were bowling along into the country.

"Do you know anything about clutches, gearboxes and accelerators?"

"Yes, I know all the theory and I've often watched other people drive; it's just that I've never had a go."

"Good – then I'll have you off in no time. This model has a beautifully smooth synchromesh gear-box, and a child could change gear."

Although I had my misgivings, I still felt a surge of excitement at the possibility of driving my own car. I gazed out of the window at the patchwork of extremely small plots of land and terraces separated by a web of dry-stone walls, and wondered why the plots were so small. While I was thinking about that, Baldy suddenly swung the jeep to the left on to a dry-stone road. We bumped and rattled for a few minutes until he stopped outside a whitewashed stone building.

"You know it must be your lucky day: not only have you been given a car, but a house as well." He pointed across to a building that I could see was surrounded by waist-high weeds. "That's where you will live, all alone, like a shepherd."

I was speechless – it was just one thing after another.

"Let's go inside," said Baldy. We got out of the jeep and pushed through the weeds to the door, and together we went inside. I discovered that there was just one room – perhaps better called a living space – with a bed with a straw palliasse and blankets folded at the head. There was also a small table and a chair and, incongruously, a red telephone.

"It's all been fitted out for you, with the walls all freshly whitewashed, and – as you can see – electric light. Why, it's a little palace!"

I was not so sure. "Is this all there is?"

"What more do you want?"

"Washing facilities, for a start."

"Oh they're all outside." He turned and guided me round the back, where I found a wooden lean-to containing a bowl and what looked like a saucepan.

"Round the corner," explained Baldy, "there's a well and you can wash in the bowl alongside. We've fitted you out with a gas ring and gas cylinder so you can even heat water for a shave."

"But where's the loo?"

"Well … there's a hut over there, but it's a trifle smelly. There is a proper toilet at the control tower, so if I were you I would control myself until I got there."

"How about meals and things?"

"I'll explain that later. Jump in and I'll show you the runway."

We drove on along the road for about 200 yards until it opened out into a full-sized airstrip.

"There you are, you see: it's quite a nice size." We drove over to one side and followed along the edge until I noticed a white cross painted on the ground. Baldy stopped the car and we both got out.

"These white crosses mark the places where a light for the flare-path must be placed." He took down one of the drums.

"You see, these are all lamps. The top is glass so that they only shine upwards and the switch is round the side. If you are ever called upon to light the flarepath, heaven forbid, then you must drive down switching every light on individually."

Baldy picked up the lamp and placed it in the car, and then together we drove on. I noticed that at the far end there was a cluster of empty dispersal points and a group of temporary buildings.

Baldy looked at me and grinned. "You see: a runway is ideal for learning to drive."

Coming to the end, he turned towards the huts and I could see men working.

"The ground crew are on detachment from Luqa. You'll see a couple of coaches going past your hut taking them back tonight. That's the motor pool there. If you have any trouble with the jeep or if you want to fill up with petrol the corporal there will sort things out, and that long building there is the dining hall where you all eat. There are no separate messes or things like that. Now we'll go to your headquarters."

The control tower was a stone farm building on the side of the runway, equidistant from either end. It looked very much like a larger version of my own hut. We drew up alongside and Baldy led the way.

"On the ground floor are the offices for the C.O. and the flight commanders. Up the stairs and you come to this large room, which will be the crew-room." I noticed that it was furnished with rather worn armchairs and a few coffee tables.

"Now," went on Baldy, "we go outside again, and round the side there are stone steps leading to the flat roof." After climbing these I discovered that the flat roof was surrounded by a stone wall about twelve inches thick and about 2 feet high. In one corner was a wooden pergola with a canvas roof, designed to protect against the sun.

"In here, you can see all your equipment. There is a V.H.F. radio set, a telephone, binoculars, two Very pistols, and packets of red and green flares. There is also a table for you to keep your log, that's that large book over there, and of course a really comfortable chair."

"That's all very well – but what do I have to do?"

"I'm sure it's a bit of a muddle for you, but it will all make sense tomorrow. Now, the squadron will be arriving about midday from an aircraft carrier lying offshore. I shall be here with you well before that. That reminds me, there is something I forgot – and that's the V.H.F. set. Now, you can see it has four frequencies controlled by those buttons there. Button B is the frequency used by Fighter Control while the planes are in flight. This doesn't concern you, but it does mean you can eavesdrop as the fighting goes on. Your frequency is on button D. You should be listening out on that all the time. Your call-sign is Brutus. Fighter Control, by the way, is Caesar. When a plane wishes to land, you will be called up using your call-sign. You will answer using his call-sign. It's as easy as that."

He looked at his watch. "Right, I'll be going back with the ground crews so that gives us a couple of hours … So let's start work on your driving lessons."

## CHAPTER SEVENTEEN

# Airfield Controller

As I sat on the parapet with Baldy, I was apprehensive about what the day had in store. It had started well with me driving us up to the control tower, for I was now sure that I could get around on my own, even if sometimes I resembled a kangaroo.

"Now, Bill, let's go over this one more time. After clearing away the lamps, you must be up here ready for action by 9 o'clock. Is that understood?" I nodded. Baldy looked at his watch.

"It's just nine now, so you can start right away. Now, take the telephone and you will find exchange will answer. Ask for Fighter Control, and he'll put you through. Then you ask for the duty controller and say:

"This is Brutus sir; the airstrip is ready for action."

Trembling a little with nerves, I did as I was told. "Thank you, Brutus", was the reply. "Your aircraft should arrive about 11 o'clock".

Baldy watched as I put down the phone.

"He says the planes will arrive about eleven."

"O.K., now all the air-crew will leave around seven at night, so that's the time when you need to lay the flare-path. It should take you about three quarters of an hour. This is important, for at 9 o'clock again you must be in your hut phoning Control to say the flarepath is ready. From that time on you must remain at the end of the phone until daybreak the next day. Is that clear?"

I nodded.

"At any time during the night, Luqa might be heavily bombed. Then you would be told, and you must dash around switching on all the lamps, and then get up to the V.H.F. set, switch on to channel D, and be prepared to land any aircraft that should be landing at Luqa."

"Do you think that is likely to happen?"

"Not really, but you must be ready in case." "Suppose there's a raid in the morning before nine?"

"There's another squadron at Takhali and they will be standing in for those periods because they live on the camp, whereas the air-crew here have to arrive by coach every morning. From all this you can see that the time between laying out the lamps and 9 o'clock is your only free time, so make the most of it."

I was not surprised to find that it was Baldy who saw them first.

"Look," he said, and pointed out four black specks in the distance. "Here they come."

It was not long before one plane roared overhead followed by another, and another, and another. The noise made my ears ring as I swung round to watch them as they swept around.

"Hello Brutus, hello Brutus, Tiger red one here, request permission to land." The message crackled over the radio. Baldy picked up the mike. "Hello Tiger red one, Brutus here. You may land at your convenience."

"Roger Brutus." One of the planes lowered its wheels and turned into the approach while Baldy picked up the Very pistol with the red cartridge.

"You must always be ready with this thing", he said, "in case the runway gets obstructed at the last minute." The Spitfire came in, floated a while, and then made a perfect landing.

Baldy was on the air immediately, "Hello Tiger red two, you can make your approach now." And so the routine went on, and soon he had brought all four aircraft down.

"So that, Bill, is how it's done. Quite simple really. Now, in 10 minutes another four will arrive, and I want you to bring them in. I'll tell you when to do everything."

I was very nervous, but I coped quite well. When the third group of four arrived, I brought them in myself without any help from Baldy. "How was that, then?"

"Fine, just remember that the moment things go pear-shaped you must send up a red signal to make the plane abort. Well, that's all

I think. Now you can manage on your own, I'll be off. I'm going to try to hitch a lift with any transport going to Luqa. Cheerio, and the best of luck."

I watched him go with trepidation, for I was not at all sure that I was up to being left. It was interesting, I thought, to look around, for everywhere was a hive of activity. Some of the planes were being refuelled while others had panels open with mechanics peering inside. I could hear raucous laughter below as the pilots fought over the best chair, and jeeps and lorries drove around like mad.

"Warrant Officer Bailey?"

I looked around to discover a squadron leader standing at the top of the steps.

"Yes, sir."

"I'm Squadron Leader Hopkins, the squadron commander. I thought I would like to introduce myself and congratulate you on the way you coped with our arrival. You are new to the game, I gather?"

"Yes, sir."

"You were an experienced captain of a Wellington, and then they all went away and left you in hospital?"

"Yes, sir."

"In that case I am sure you will have no problems here. Now, this afternoon I intend to have a meeting with the pilots downstairs, and I thought I would like to hear your views first. Was there anything that struck you as being in need of improvement?"

I felt proud to be consulted, and remembered two things that had struck me.

"Well, sir, the first thing I noticed was the importance of leaving the runway quickly after landing. If a plane dawdles around, there is a risk to the next aircraft."

"Good – I'll mention that. Anything else?"

"Well, I know nothing about Spitfires – but I was wondering, sir, if you came over the perimeter wall just a little low, then how much of the runway would you need for your landing?"

The C.O. studied it carefully.

"About two thirds I should think; at a push, a half."

"Then I could allow planes to land while others are still on the runway? I can imagine that if you had been on an op you would all want to get down as quick as possible."

"Yes, that's true. I think you could allow them to land as they saw fit, but always be ready to give out a signal to overshoot. Now, Bailey, the important bit. With your experience I am sure you will have no difficulty. As from tomorrow we shall be part of the battle plan, and we will always have a section of four aircraft at 10-minute readiness. Now, you see that area there at the beginning of the runway? That will be where the four planes will wait. All the time they will have pilots in the cockpits, starter batteries and mechanics by their side. Now, the moment Control phone you and say, "Scramble four," then you must fire a green star into the air. Is that clear?" I nodded.

"Good – then off they go, and although they will be on 10-minute readiness, I want them in the air in 5 minutes. Understood?"

"Yes, sir, I'll do my best."

"Now, the next four aircraft will be on 30-minute readiness. The pilots will be in the crew room, but as soon as they hear the others taking off they will make their way to their aircraft. Then they will move up to take the place of the airborne section. It may happen that you will be given instructions to scramble another four almost on top of the other, and then you must fire a second green signal, and do everything you can to get them safely airborne."

"Yes, sir. What happens if an aircraft comes in damaged?"

"That won't happen because the plane will be diverted to Luqa. They have all the workshops there."

"And supposing a plane comes in and does a belly landing on the runway?"

"Then you phone Control tell them what has happened and they will divert everyone to either Luqa or Takhali. Anything else?"

"No, sir."

"Good show, I think I can have confidence in you." He turned away and went down the steps and left me to digest everything I had heard. Perhaps, I thought, the senior controller had been right and I did have an important part to play.

There was no flying that afternoon, so I could sit on the parapet and watch everything that was going on. The fire tender crew were unrolling their hoses and checking for flaws; the mechanics were cleaning their charges, some polishing their perspex canopies, while others were changing oil and refuelling the aircraft … and so, when it happened, it was quite a shock. I knew it would happen, but I was unprepared for it in reality. At exactly 7 o'clock the first coach left, followed by the other three. I looked around nervously, for the crew room was quiet, still and empty, and as far as I could see there was not a soul.

"Hi down there," I shouted, to break the silence; but no one answered.

What had Baldy said? "Get the flare-path out, and then the time's your own until 9 o'clock."

I descended the steps and strolled over to the motor pool where I had parked the jeep, now and again looking over my shoulder to see if I was being followed, for the place had taken on an eerie atmosphere. I turned the ignition key and started the engine. This is it, I thought, this is for real.

It took me about half an hour and then I drove down the road and parked it beside my hut. I went inside and looked around; for now I was on my own I could move things about as I wished. I moved the table, I sat in the chair, I slid the telephone over until it was near my right hand, I switched the electric bulb on and off, and finally felt that it was all really mine. Then I went outdoors and inspected the lean-to. It was much nicer than I had at first thought, the roof being festooned with grapevines with bunches of very small white grapes hanging down. I tasted some and found that, although small with tough skins, they were very sweet. I looked up and could see the sun setting in a riot of reds and oranges. I went inside and laid on my bed. There was no doubt that time was going to hang heavily on my hands.

Although the hands of my watch seemed never to move, yet it gradually came to 9 o'clock. I picked up the telephone and the operator answered.

"Can I have Fighter Control please?"

"Fighter Control – sure."

There was a click and a voice answered, "Duty controller."

"This is Brutus, sir, the flare-path is available."

"Very good." I replaced the phone, and that was that. I hoped that I would not have to use it again, and so when the phone rang half an hour later I was horrified.

I picked up the phone and put it to my ear.

"Hi there, operator here. Steve's the name, are you on duty all night?"

"Yes."

"Where are you?"

"I'm in a shepherd's hut on the airstrip."

"You must be bored out of your mind."

"It's my first night, and I guess you're right."

"Tell you what – how about listening to the Forces Programme?"

"Haven't a radio."

"That's O.K. I'll feed it through the phone. I've got to be here all night and I always have it on for me."

"But suppose someone wants to call me?"

"Then I'll just put the squealer on, and that would wake the dead."

"Could you do that?"

"Sure thing. Place the headset in a bowl or bucket and you should be able to hear it reasonably well."

"I shan't be able to contact you ..."

"That's true, but I'll come on line and listen every hour. So here goes." There were a few clicks and soon the strains of Glenn Miller could be heard through the phone.

A few days later, I was in the middle of laying the flare-path. I straightened up after placing a lamp in position when a flash of white attracted my attention. I thought this strange, and after completing my task I drove over to the dining room to investigate.

"Anyone there?" I called. The door opened and one of the cooks appeared.

"What are you doing here? The coaches went ages ago."

"I'm the duty chef."

"I didn't know there was such a thing."

"Switch off that engine and come inside."

I left the jeep and followed the cook inside into the kitchen.

"The pilots come here straight from their billets and so they need breakfast first thing, so every night one of us has to stay so that the breakfast is ready for when they arrive."

"I thought I was the only one here at night," I replied.

"I didn't know you were here either."

"I have to be on the end of the phone from 9 o'clock onwards. Why don't you come over when you've finished and listen to the radio."

"You've got a radio?"

"Well, not exactly – but the operator puts it through my phone."

So began a relationship that was the only thing that kept me sane. Sometimes they would bring some coffee, or dry tea, and once a can of white powder that was labelled Klim that I realised was the word "milk" spelt backwards. Even more welcome, they would bring a bacon sandwich that had been pilfered from the air-crews' breakfast ration.

Sometimes the cook, who was off duty on Wednesday, would come over with the others in the coach and join me in a day's tour of the island. Sometimes we would visit the church in Rabat and wonder at the vast dome, with its hole where once, during mass, a bomb fell through, landing on the stone floor without hurting a single soul. The worshippers were sure it was a miracle, but really it was just a dud bomb. Sometimes we would sit and look out to sea at the little island of Gozo, and sometimes we would visit the other end of the island to Valletta and stand shocked at all the damage done to the Opera House.

The squadron received its baptism of fire from the first day. As per the squadron commander's orders, the four planes that were on 10-minute readiness had taxied out and were ready at the beginning of the runway, each plane with its own mechanic, starter battery and pilot. At seven minutes past nine I received the order to scramble four. I released a green signal, and the four planes were in the air in 4 minutes. The planes that were on 30 minutes now had to be prepared; the pilots left the crew room chatting among themselves as they made their way to the dispersals. However, they were startled to see that I had released a second signal telling them to take off immediately. This led to frantic activity, for although they had 30 minutes to be ready for flight, the earlier they were airborne the better. The squadron commander was probably pleased, as they were all in the air inside 12 minutes.

Serviceability was 100% as they were new to the island, and so the remaining four aircraft were immediately made ready and moved up to the end of the runway in readiness. By then, however, the first planes were returning, so I had to take care to ensure that the runway was free when they wanted to land.

The day carried on in this frenetic fashion as the battle for Malta was fought. The next day was the same, but by the third day the pressure was beginning to ease, and on the fourth day the section on 10-minute readiness was not scrambled at all.

Days became weeks, weeks became months, and life settled down to air tests and an occasional scramble. The Spitfires' role began to change from a defensive one to one of attack. They were fitted with bomb releases on each wing and would take off with one 250-pound bomb under each wing to look for a train, convoy of lorries, or anything that might disrupt the enemy's war effort.

One night I was all alone listening to the radio over the phone when the music was suddenly replaced by a loud screech. I picked up the phone.

"Exchange, you have a call."

"Brutus here," I answered.

"Duty controller here. I have fresh orders for you. Are you ready to concentrate?"

Puzzled, I replied, "Yes, sir."

"Right, your squadron will be leaving for another airbase tomorrow. The squadron commander has been informed. At 10:00 hours a D.C.3 Dakota aircraft will leave Luqa. It will climb to 3,000 feet and then circle over Qrendi. When you see the aircraft, you are to give the order for them to take off. They will all be ready by then. Is that clear?"

"Yes, sir. Where are they going?"

"Top secret, I'm afraid. Goodnight."

Next day was full of excitement, for all the ground crews by now were in the know, and the strip was full of the roar of engines being warmed up, while others were being fuelled for what seemed to be a long journey. All pilots had arrived at their dispersals and soon the first plane was edging on to the runway. Slowly it taxied forward to be followed by all the others, until every plane was queuing up along the edge of the runway.

The senior mechanic appeared on the roof.

"Can I come up?" he asked. I nodded, and soon the roof was full of N.C.O.s eager to see their charges fly away.

I was concentrating on the sky. I was not sure … was it? Yes: I was sure a twin-engined aircraft was climbing away on the horizon. I watched as it levelled out and turned toward me. Soon the plane was overhead – and now I was sure, because it began turning slowly round. I picked up my microphone.

"Hello all Tiger aircraft, Brutus here: off you go, and the best of luck." For the last time I fired a Very light, its green star sailing into the sky. There was a cheer from the crowd and a waving of arms as the planes turned and roared off down the runway.

It was a sombre crowd that descended the steps.

The last view they had had was of the Spitfires in formation following the Dakota that contained the navigator for the whole group, getting smaller and smaller as they flew away.

I slumped in my chair, quite tired after all the tension. I wondered whether there would be much work for me now. The ground crews were packing all their equipment away and transport was moving around ready to take everything back to Luqa. I wondered whether I should contact Control when the phone rang.

"Is that Warrant Officer Bailey?"

"Yes, sir."

"This is the senior controller, do you remember me?"

"Yes, sir."

"Well, Bailey, I have decided to take Qrendi out of commission. You have done some good work, but I have a final job for you to do. I want you to go back to your quarters and pack your kit. Pile it into your jeep and drive to the airfield at Luqa. Can you do that?"

"Yes, sir."

"Good, then I want you to park it outside the control tower. On the ground floor you will find the transport officer's office. Report in there and hand over the ignition keys of the jeep, as you will not be needing it again."

He hesitated, leaving me to wonder what my next job was.

"The transport officer will then hand over your travelling documents. You have been posted back to the U.K."

## CHAPTER EIGHTEEN

# UK

Although it had taken months for me to fly to the Middle East, it only took 3 days to fly home. One stop in Tunisia, a change of plane in Algeria, and now I was looking around in the concourse of Prestwick airport.

I was funnelled into an office where an army clerk sat at a desk. "Where are you bound, sir?" he asked.

"U.K."

"You're in the U.K.," he said, in a bored voice.

I smiled. "I'm sorry," I said, "But I've been telling that to officials all the way."

"Where have you been posted, sir?"

"I've no idea."

"In that case, you are due for leave. Where shall I make the warrant out to?"

I thought for a moment. "Newbury," I said.

"Right – and if you give me your pay-book, I'll issue you with some back pay."

The journey home was a nightmare. The trains did not arrive on time, and when they did they were packed. In spite of this, every time they stopped at a station the platform would be four or five people deep along its whole length. The doors would be wrenched open and even more lucky people would be pushed in, so that when it drew away the train would be so full that it was impossible to move. I spent the journey sitting on my luggage in the corridor, and the soldier who had taken residence in the toilet was never once disturbed.

The problem arose when someone wanted to leave. It was necessary to start sidling and edging around bodies to reach the door a long time in advance, so that when the train stopped people were in the right position. Many found that they were taken past their stop because they didn't prepare in advance.

I found the journey endless, and it wasn't helped by a 2-hour wait outside Euston while the line was repaired.

It was nice to see Dad again. I thought he looked unchanged, and was very smart in the uniform of a sergeant in the Home Guard. I knew that I ought to be pleased to be home, but the fact was that I had a splitting headache.

"Are you alright, son?" asked Dad.

"To tell you the truth, I have a bit of a headache." He got up and placed a hand on my forehead.

"You do look flushed, and you seem to have a bit of a fever. It's probably a touch of the 'flu, there's a lot of it about just now."

I would normally have dismissed it, but since my bout of malaria I was a little nervous about fevers.

"If I was on camp, I would go and see the M.O."

"There's an R.A.F. station near here. Would you like to go there?" my father enquired, but before I could answer I collapsed on to the sofa.

"I'm going to phone the R.A.F. and get them to send someone."

"You can't do that – they don't have their phones listed in the telephone directory."

"I have an idea. I'll be back in a minute." He wheeled his bike into the road and cycled away.

True to his word, he was back in 10 minutes.

"They're going to send an ambulance soon."

I looked up. "How did you manage that?"

"I'm Chairman of the Dig for Victory Committee, and I have a contact up there."

The orderlies were very kind and helped me into the ambulance. "We've got to take you to the sickbay," they said.

The M.O. was waiting and he gave me a thorough examination.

"You've got a high temperature, so we won't take any chances. It's probably malaria, so we'll keep you here overnight and send you off to hospital in the morning."

That night seemed endless to me, as I tossed and turned in delirium. I was in bed at R.A.F. Greenham Common. But I couldn't be, because Greenham Common was a golf course. Many were the times when I had spent a Saturday morning scrambling for golf balls. The course, I remembered, used large gorse bushes for bunkers, and golfers were very reluctant to venture too close. I remembered, too, often cycling to my grandparents and using the golf course as a short cut. How could it possibly be an aerodrome? As the night wore on I was conscious of the roar of aircraft and I started dreaming of the raid in Malta. I jumped up with a shout and an orderly came in, wiped my forehead and gave me a drink of cold water.

I remembered being taken to the ambulance on a stretcher, and the vibration as they drove along, but I must have slept for most of the way, for when I looked up a nurse was preparing to take my temperature.

"Hello," she said, "Now you are Mr. Bailey, is that right? I'm Sarah, and I shall be here during the day." It all seemed very comfortable to me, in fact my headache seemed to be getting better and the next day when the doctor and matron made their rounds I was sitting up and looking about.

The doctor scanned the notes at the foot of my bed. "Well, you seem to be on the mend already. Your temperature is dropping. I don't know exactly what caused that flare-up. We do know that it was not malaria. If you keep on getting better, then we'll keep you in for a week because you are very malnourished, not much more than skin and bone. We'll feed you on a special rich diet, and with the bed rest it should get you fit again."

It seemed an ideal holiday for me, and on the third day I was sitting in the sun reading the newspaper and looking forward to my meal of cauliflower cheese, rich creamy rice pudding and a glass of Guinness.

On the fourth day, Sarah came and took my temperature and looked concerned. "It's up a little, Bill. Perhaps you overdid it yesterday. Stay in bed this morning until I've seen Sister."

Twelve hours later, I had a high temperature and was lying in bed with a fan continuously trying to get my fever down.

And so the pattern continued. Next day I was on the mend and 2 days later I was up and about, only to be followed by another relapse, to be followed by another period of normality. It was during one of my spells out of bed that I looked up to find an air commodore approaching, followed by a flock of flight lieutenants.

"Bailey," he said, "You've given us quite a problem. However, at last we've cracked it. You are suffering from a rare form of relapsing fever, quite common in North Africa. We will wait until your next attack and then we'll give you some tablets, and that will be that."

And so I waited for over 3 weeks without any signs of a relapse. Eventually, when the doctor did his round, he studied my chart and said, "I don't think we can wait much longer. The only thing I can think of is that we have built up your constitution until your natural immune system has been able to overcome it. I feel we've got to get rid of you. There are a few routine tests to do, and then we must say goodbye. What do you think about that?"

I wasn't sure what I felt. I had enjoyed the rest, but nevertheless it would be good to get home.

And so they took samples of blood, samples of urine, and samples of my stool, while I began to pack my few possessions ready for home.

Next day a male nurse approached: "Mr Bailey?" I nodded.

"I've got a disappointment for you. You will not be going home just yet, for you have contracted amoebic dysentery and we've got to get rid of that first. So if you'll just get back into bed I'll be along in 10 minutes to start the treatment."

"How long will it take?"

"The whole treatment will take 10 days, and then – all being well – you'll be allowed to go home."

I did as I was told, although I couldn't understand why I had to get into bed just to take a tablet and so I was astonished when the orderly returned pushing a loaded trolley. He pushed it right up to the bed and drew the curtains round.

"The treatment consists of colonic irrigation every day for 10 days."

"What does that mean?" I looked on anxiously as the orderly picked up a long rubber tube.

"It means that I have to pass this rubber tube up your back passage. Then we'll wash out your bowel until it's as clean as a new pin."

I was told to lie on my side and suffer the indignity of the rubber tube. Attached to the other end was a funnel that the orderly lifted above the height of the bed. He then poured warm water into the funnel and held it high until gradually gravity forced the water into my interior. When it was all gone the funnel was lowered, allowing the water to pour out into a bowl. The whole process was repeated over and over again until the orderly was satisfied that the water was coming out clean.

"That's fine," he said, "Now comes the difficult part for you. You see this bright yellow liquid? I'm going to fill the funnel and pass it into your bowel." He held the funnel high and filled it with about half a pint of brilliant fluorescent yellow disinfectant.

"Now, Mr Bailey, I am going to remove the tube and it's up to you to keep that liquid in for at least an hour. Then you can go to the lavatory and get rid of it. You'll find you have to consciously keep your sphincter muscle tight, or you will be staining the bed and Sister will not be amused. Stay in bed and think of nothing else and you'll be all right."

That first hour seemed endless, but with each treatment it became easier and the stain on my sheet became smaller. Ten days later I was declared fit and was allowed to return home.

I was disappointed, but not surprised, when I failed my air-crew medical. I wondered what they would do with me this time. After all I had been left alone in Malta, and then I had been given an airfield to control, but that was not likely here, and after all there were few jobs going for a grounded pilot. When my posting came through, I was intrigued to discover that I had to report to Abingdon as a Link trainer instructor.

A Link trainer was the very first flight simulator. It consisted of a cockpit complete with all controls and instrument panel, contained in an imitation plane. This plane was balanced on four bellows mounted on a rotating turntable. By passing air into and out of the bellows, the plane could climb, dive, and bank to the left or right. The pupil sat in the cockpit with a hood pulled down, thus depriving him of any visual signals about what the plane was doing.

One of the earliest lessons was to sit the pupil in the cockpit and ask him to fly straight and level. After a while his instruments were switched off and the hood dropped down. Almost inevitably a wing would slowly drop, making the plane bank and turn, and this would become more and more extreme until the plane was spinning round and round. While this was going on we would ask the pupil if he was quite happy flying straight and level. The pupil would then lift the hood and find to his astonishment that in actual fact he was spinning round.

"So you see," I would say, "you must never rely on your feelings, for they can let you down. You must always rely on your instruments."

I would sit at the instructor's desk. This had a complete facsimile of the pupil's instrument panel so that I could see exactly the height, speed and compass direction of the little plane. The desk was really a glasstopped table on top of which was a piece of machinery nicknamed "the crab". This travelled over the table drawing a red line that showed the track of the simulator.

Sometimes I would ask the pupil to fly due north for 5 minutes, then east for 5 minutes, then south and then west. If this was done perfectly the crab would draw a square ending up exactly at the starting point. Further more complicated manoeuvres followed, making the crab draw patterns like Maltese crosses and other things.

I found it all great fun; but soon I became very, very bored and so was thrilled when at the next medical I passed A1. Now, at last, I could again fly my very own plane.

## CHAPTER NINETEEN

# Staff Navigator

The ways of the Postings Department of the Air Ministry were impossible to fathom. I was on leave when the letter arrived, and I read it with surprise. I had been posted to the Empire Central Navigation School at Shawbury. Well, I thought, someone had to fly the students around, but then I read the letter more closely and discovered that I had been posted to No. 32 Staff Navigators Course. I was not a pilot, but a student!

Shawbury was really the University of Air Navigation, and staff navigators ran the navigation departments at airfields and provided instructors for air-crew in Training Command. But why should I, a pilot, be posted to a course like that? There was no doubt that they would find out their mistake soon; but in the meantime, I just had to do as I was told.

When I arrived at Shawbury the situation became even more ridiculous. There were ten students on my course, all of them commissioned officers with navigational experience. As the only non-commissioned rank I just had the same accommodation as the others, and so it was the first time in my life that I had a servant to make my bed and tidy my room. The others on the course were very kind to me and were only too pleased to help me, and all did their best to make certain that I came through the course.

The course consisted of lectures on plotting, astronomy, meteorology, and an introduction into radar. Radar was then becoming important in navigation, and so we had to know all about cathode-ray tubes and how it was possible to measure ridiculously small time intervals with an oscilloscope. We were taught how to use the system code-named "G", the long-range system "Loran", and the hush-hush system called "H2S".

The practical work was centred on plotting exercises in the classroom, as well as in their equivalent of the Link trainer. Each student was placed in a cubicle and given the task of navigating himself around a course. Every now and again, slips of paper were handed in giving information needed to carry on. All this was carried out in real time, the only problem being that the real time was based on a clock visible to all, and this had been doctored to work three times faster than normal. This meant, of course, that in 2 hours we were expected to fly a trip of 6 hours.

I worked hard and was thrilled when I passed all the examinations, in fact coming second in meteorology, and so was posted as a fully-fledged staff navigator to run the navigation department at R.A.F. Penrhos.

1 soon discovered that this was quite an easy option. As it was a school for air gunners, navigation did not rate high on their list of requirements, so apart from loaning out copies of the local Ordnance Survey map sheet there was little else to do. As a matter of form, I made sure that I always had in the office a copy of the latest weather report; this meant frequent visits to the station met office.

There was one young lady there with whom I enjoyed having a chat. I admired her expertise in plotting the weather chart. She would go into the teleprinter room and return with yards of paper covered with rows and rows of figures. She would then pick up two pens that had been fixed together with rubber bands, dip one into red ink and the other into black ink, and proceed to translate the numbers into symbols grouped around first one met station and then another, until the map was full and complete. She would then mark on the isobars and possible fronts, leaving it for the forecaster to use in his forecast. She was often there alone, and often throughout the night, so I began to spend many a happy hour with her. I was not much of a ladies' man, in fact girls had not been of much interest: and yet I found increasingly my thoughts would wander to what she was doing and whether I would see her that night.

One evening I popped in, and was worried when I saw her obviously frightened.

"Gwen, whatever's happened? You look as if you've seen a ghost."

She gave a weak smile. "Nothing, really – I had to go out in the dark to read the instruments, which you know I have to do every hour, and I was just shutting the screen when right behind me an old man gave a cough."

"A man, was he following you or something?"

"No it wasn't a man, it was a sheep. But it was so realistic it really frightened me."

"You shouldn't go out there alone."

"Nonsense! – it's part of my job." She busied herself with copying her readings into the log.

But there was something on my mind … I didn't know whether I had the courage to mention it; and then, as she turned round smiling, I said, "Gwen, you know it will soon be Christmas? I was wondering if you would come to Caernarvon with me to do some Christmas shopping. We could leave on the Friday afternoon, spend the night in a hotel, and then spend the rest of the day round the shops. What do you say?"

As soon as I said it I regretted it, for I could see from her face that she was shocked.

"Don't get me wrong," I hastened to say, "We would of course have separate rooms and we would meet again at breakfast."

I watched as she quickly gathered the two coffee cups and started washing them at the sink. She dried first one and then the other; then, looking at me, she said, "I would like that."

Apart from the fact that the hotel was next door to a milk-bottling plant, which meant noise at five in the morning, the visit was a great success and as we sat together in the bus going home it was only natural that I should put my arm around her. She snuggled in to me and I kissed her hair and squeezed her tight.

Gradually we grew more and more fond of each other, and there came a time when I knew from the rota that she would have the next Sunday off and so I planned to share it with her. It therefore came as a dreadful shock when she told me that she couldn't see me because she had another date.

I was stunned, but of course it was quite possible that she had had boyfriends before I had come along; and so, with as good a grace as I could muster, I wished her every happiness.

I stayed away for three whole days because I didn't want to get in the way, but eventually I could not stand it any longer, so opened the door and went in. Gwen was studying the chart and as she looked up she said, "Hello, stranger – what have you been doing all this while?"

"I didn't want to see you with your old love. I thought I couldn't stand it."

"Whatever are you talking about?

"The man you spent Sunday with."

"Oh Bill, don't tell me you're jealous."

"Well, I suppose I am."

"Then there's no need. Look." She pulled open a drawer and took out a bulging notebook. "This is my 'old love', as you call it," and held out the book.

"Don't tell me you have a book of phone numbers?"

"Read it."

I took the book and turned the pages; I studied a few, and then looked at her in astonishment. "I don't understand."

"What do you think it is?"

"It looks as if you've been writing about Bible texts or something."

"That is my 'old love'." Gwen laughed, "Let me put you out of your misery. In Pwllheli there is a little chapel. For the last year I have been keeping it going. I run the Sunday school and often take the services, and generally do anything that needs doing. So you see I couldn't go out with you because it was a Sunday."

I took her in my arms and kissed her. "I'm sorry I was such a fool", I said.

Gradually I became more and more obsessed with her, until I found myself thinking about her all the time. I hummed to myself as I went about my work, and it was no doubt obvious to all that I was in love. I felt that Gwen loved me, and yet sometimes when she thought I was not looking, she looked sad.

Darling, is there anything wrong? Sometimes you look so unhappy. Have I done anything?"

She looked up and I was surprised to find her eyes were full of tears.

I took her in my arms. "There, there, it can't be all that bad. What's it all about?"

"It's my mother; she insists that I must stop seeing you. She feels that I should wait until after the war, and then I could find a real boyfriend at home."

"That's ridiculous; surely you are old enough to make up your own mind?"

"Yes, I know; but I've never gone against her wishes."

As time went by, I could see that this seriously troubled Gwen and so I decided to act. One weekend, without saying anything to anyone, I used the local train to catch the Holyhead express from Bangor. It took all night to travel down to Euston, and by the time I had used the underground to Victoria, a stopping train to Brighton, and another to Worthing, it was gone ten on the Sunday morning. A passer-by directed me to the house which was a mile and a half away. I walked along wondering what I was going to say, but when I got near I saw a lady with a prayer book and her husband leaving the house, obviously on their way to church. They paused for a moment to discuss their flower border, giving me enough time to approach.

"Excuse me ... Mrs. Bates?"

The lady gave me a stern look. "Yes?"

"My name is Bailey, and I've come down to tell you about your daughter."

The lady looked quickly at her husband. "I think you had better come in."

She turned and unlocked the door, then ushering me into the lounge she said, "You'd better sit there while I take off my coat."

A few minutes later, they both returned and sat opposite me on the other side of the dining-room table.

She looked at me carefully without saying a word and then, "Am I right in thinking that you are the young man who has been seeing my daughter?"

I nodded.

"I see." There was another awkward pause. "Well, what did you want to see us about?"

"I've come to tell you how your actions are upsetting your daughter.

"Really."

"Yes, I know you love your daughter and that she loves you, however she has told me that you have forbidden her to see me and this is splitting her apart. She loves you and wants to please you and yet she loves me too, and so this is putting her in torment."

"Forbidding is perhaps too strong a term – I only want the best for her."

"I'm sure you do. Well, I must go now."

Gwen's father joined in, "Now son, what do you mean to do after the war?"

I turned towards him. "The crew I once flew with, sir, said that that was one question that should never be asked, but if I'm still alive, God willing, I thought I would like to try my hand at teaching."

"Just a minute," said her mother, "have you come all this way just to say that?"

"Yes, because I am sure that once you know the position you will not put your daughter through such agony."

"I won't ask you whether you love my daughter, because that is obvious; but does she love you, and are you both serious about each other?"

"I'm sure she does, and we have never been more serious about anything."

"Then after you've gone, we must think about this."

On the way home, I thought what a fool I had been. I had acted without thought and had probably made things worse. After all, meeting one's possible mother-in-law after travelling all night in a train, without a wash or even a shave, was hardly likely to impress.

It was 2 days before I could pluck up enough courage to visit the met office. Gwen was plotting a map. She glanced up. "Hello," she said, "Where have you been?"

I stood just behind her, "I've been chatting to your mum."

"Rubbish, she's not on the phone." "No, I went to talk to her."

Gwen stopped her work and looked up in astonishment. "You went all the way down to Worthing?"

I nodded, noticing her two pens were pointed at me like poison darts.

"Oh Bill, what have you done?"

"It was just that I hated to see you so upset, and I thought if perhaps she knew how she was worrying her daughter she would not do it."

"Hang on, I must finish this chart and then you must tell me all about it."

I made us two cups of coffee. I felt I needed it, because I didn't need her to tell me that I had been a fool, and after she had heard my account I could see that not only did she wonder this, but was also worried about what would happen next.

"Well; it's done now – we must just make the best of it." She fumbled in a drawer, pulled out a hanky and blew her nose.

"I am sorry, darling, I was only trying to help and now it seems I have made things worse."

Two pilots came in for forecasts, and so it was not possible to continue the conversation.

"Must go, see you tomorrow."

It was lunchtime next day before I saw her again. I had hung around outside until the forecaster had left, and when I was fairly sure she was on her own I tapped timidly on the door and went in. To my surprise, Gwen dashed to me and threw her arms around my neck. "It's all right my darling, she approves."

"Who does?"

"Mum. It seems that she has thought over what you said and has written to say that she was only thinking of me and that perhaps it was time for me to make my own decisions and that she wouldn't stand in our way."

"Did she say anything about me?"

"Yes; she said you were obviously in love, but she also thought you were crazy. Still, it seems that what clinched it was when you said you wanted to go into teaching. You didn't tell me that."

"It's an idea I've had recently."

"You see, Mum was a teacher, and so that was a point in your favour." She danced around the office. "You don't know what a relief all this is!"

I caught her, looked into her eyes, and then, taking her hand, kissed it. "Darling, will you marry me?"

"Of course, dear, of course I will."

The halcyon days that followed were short-lived, for much to my annoyance I was sent to an airfield at Llandurog to run the office there. Llandurog was only a 5-minute bus ride from Caernarvon, but unfortunately over an hour from Pwllheli. When I arrived I found that I was expected to share a hut with nine other men, and after having had my own room for so long this was too much. I decided to stay in Caernarvon, and so rented a room in a small commercial hotel in the town.

It was rather nice to catch the bus every evening into town, and I could kid myself that I was a civilian doing an ordinary job. It had its drawbacks in the morning, for I had to get up at six.

Early in the morning it was often dark and dismal.

All the shops were shut and Castle Square was deserted. Festooned across the square were wires holding electric bulbs in the bottoms of empty paint tins. These shone a little circle of light straight downwards, and as the wind caused the wires to sway, so the circles of light moved over the dark and empty buses. The only light came from the window of a transport cafe. It was impossible to see inside, for the window dripped with condensation; however, I opened the door and went in. The place was packed with airmen. Behind the counter, a beefy-looking man with anchors tattooed on his arms was pouring tea. Before him he had a metal tray packed with mugs. Picking up a teapot as big as a watering can, he sprayed tea over all the mugs, filling them – as well as the tray – with tea.

I sat at a table dirty with rings from countless mugs until suddenly there was a mad dive for the door. The first bus for camp was about to leave.

Whenever she could, Gwen came over on the bus.

Then we would sit holding hands in the "snug" looking at the ancient gas fire and listening to its hissing and occasional pop, until one evening the landlord tapped on the door.

"Sorry to bother you two love-birds, but I was wondering whether you might be interested in some rings? A friend of mine is in the bar, and he has some you might like to see." We looked at each other and nodded.

The landlord left to return with a seedy-looking man in a long overcoat. This man produced about half a dozen ring boxes from his voluminous pockets. He opened them and displayed them for Gwen to see. Being wartime, it was very difficult to find jewellery of any description; Gwen was thrilled to be able to try so many on. One caught her interest and so it was bought, the deal was celebrated with a glass of Madeira, and she left for camp with an engagement ring of which she was proud.

In the past I thought of postings as times of new beginnings, with new opportunities, but now when a posting came through I was furious. As soon as I had become engaged I was being posted right across the country, to the east, to Peterborough. Leaving Gwen behind, and promising to write often, I packed my bags and was off.

CHAPTER TWENTY

# The End of the War

Idiscovered that Peterborough was a comfortable little pre-war aerodrome situated only 5 minutes' walk from the railway station and city centre. It seemed to exist in a time-warp: conditions on camp were the same as before the war. Even now it was not engaged in the war, because it was being used as an elementary flying school for Frenchmen who one day would be the pilots of a new French air force.

I was told to report to the chief ground instructor, who told me that I had been posted there to lecture on meteorology; in fact, I was to be responsible for the subject right through to the cadets' final exams. This was a wonderful opportunity because, with the civilian approach of the school generally, it was like teaching in a polytechnic. In fact I thoroughly enjoyed my job, and I became more convinced than ever that teaching would be the career for me.

I had just taken my last class one afternoon when I was called to the C.G.I.'s office.

"Warrant Officer Bailey, may I introduce Flight Lieutenant Stubbs. He is the commanding officer of the A.T.C. unit that is camped at the far end of the field. He tells me that his cadets are supposed to be given air experience while they are at camp, and wonders whether we can help. Now, we have one Anson aircraft in the maintenance hangar that could be used for such a purpose. However, we need a pilot; and it appears that you are the only pilot on camp to have been cleared for twin-engine aircraft. Would you agree to take these kids for a trip round?"

I jumped at the chance, thinking it would be good to get into the air again, and so on my next free day I decided to try the old Anson out.

Having done the usual cockpit checks I taxied out to the edge of the field, and then turning into wind I opened both throttles and felt the old thrill coming back as it accelerated across the grass. However, very soon another, less welcome, familiar feeling returned: halfway across the field, I realised I was never going to make it.

Due to a combination of circumstances, I was sure I would never get off the ground. First, the light wind meant that I needed a longer run; second, the plane was old and did not have the zip of a new aircraft; and third, the take-off area was a small grass field that was suitable for elementary lightweight planes but hardly big enough for a twin-engine aeroplane. To top it all, it was only then that I realised that along the edge of the field ran the main railway line embankment.

I gripped the control column with white knuckles and could feel the familiar adrenalin rush lift the hair on the back of my head, as I stared at the rapidly approaching embankment.

Keeping the plane straight with the rudder, I kept a steady pressure back on the control column, sensing the resistance of the control surfaces against the slipstream. Gradually it became stronger and I felt it might fly, so a little stronger pressure and the plane became unstuck ... at last I staggered over the embankment with inches to spare.

Unfortunately I was not yet "out of the woods", because I found myself flying straight into a collection of tall chimneys belonging to the London Brick Works. To my horror, there was one straight ahead; so, although only now travelling a little faster than stalling speed, I banked and turned, just missed it, and slowly climbed above the next, passing over it so close that I could see down its gaping sooty interior.

The rest of the circuit was uneventful and I landed normally, noticing as I did so that the plane required ten strokes of the pump to get the flaps fully down.

That, I knew, had been too close for comfort; but as I taxied round I remembered having found a way around a similar situation. It had been in Gibraltar and I had been told to take off with a very heavily loaded Wellington bomber from the rather short runway. I had been shown a tip that took yards off the take-off run, so I decided to give it one more try. I taxied around to the downwind edge of the field and, turning round as close to the hedge as I could, I turned into wind. Carefully I locked my brakes on full and then slowly opened up the throttles. The plane shook and vibrated as the engines achieved full power; soon the tail was bumping up and down as the aircraft strained against the brakes. Suddenly I released the brakes and the plane lurched into life. She bounded across the grass like an excited dog released from its lead, and I was airborne with one third of the field to spare.

However, in bed that night I had serious misgivings. Was there enough power to take off with a load of six boys? Should I take the risk? The boys would be in my care, and the parents did not expect their children to be in danger. But if I cancelled, the kids would be very disappointed. I tossed and turned, worrying about what to do. After all, the last take-off had been normal; but with six boys? If one of the boys had been my son, would I allow him to go? I just couldn't make up my mind. In the end, I decided, perhaps it would be O.K. after all.

Early next morning, I popped into the Met Office and had a quick look at the prebaratic chart. This showed a forecast of pressure systems across the Atlantic. I smiled, for it was as I remembered: a whole family of depressions were approaching. This meant that the still conditions would be replaced by a stiff wind; and – what was more important – this would be coming from the opposite direction. So when I took the boys for their trip, I took off away from the embankment, the wind meant a shorter take-off: the only things in the way were the perimeter hedge and, after 100 yards, two rows of council houses.

All the boys enjoyed their initiation. They looked down at the city with its cathedral and its river, and they flew east where the flat fens stretched to the horizon, the black soil being divided with ruler-like efficiency by the silver drainage ditches and canals. They were excited by the approach – which was safe, though close – to the yawning mouths of the chimneys, although the chimneys were not noticed by them all, for the undercarriage needed fifty turns of a wheel before it was locked down.

Unknown to me, that would be the last time I would ever pilot my own plane; for events were proceeding rapidly abroad. The

Allies had swept across Europe, Hitler had committed suicide and Admiral Karl Doenitz unconditionally surrendered on May in 1945.

The next day, May 8th, was declared V.E. Day; and Peterborough set out to celebrate. By the evening, the streets were packed with people. The Salvation Army band marched up and down, while a few streets away the city silver band gave spirited renderings of their summer fete repertoire, and from every shop doorway came the sound of Vera Lynn singing "There'll Always be an England". All the pubs remained open, and although most had run out of beer early on, beer was not necessary, for everyone was drunk on euphoria. Every now and then the crowd would dissolve to show circles of dancers going back and forth in the steps of the hokey-cokey, while snakes of conga dancers moved sinuously through the crowds, the people at the back having no idea who was in the lead; the snakes grew longer and longer as solitary people joined on to take their share in the fun.

All the wooden frames of the market stalls were taken down and used to fuel the giant bonfire, and the French cadets spent their time in moving the mess piano outside onto the roof of the orderly room.

It had been a long time in coming, but now we all could look to a future.

I, Mr. S. Bailey, retired teacher, closed my computer and thought about what I had written. Perhaps I *had* been lucky in the past, but what I knew for certain was that despite arthritis, two false knees, two hearing aids, and false teeth, I was really lucky now. For it was my 58th wedding anniversary; and the family, daughters, grandchildren, and great-grandchild were coming to help us celebrate.

*The End*